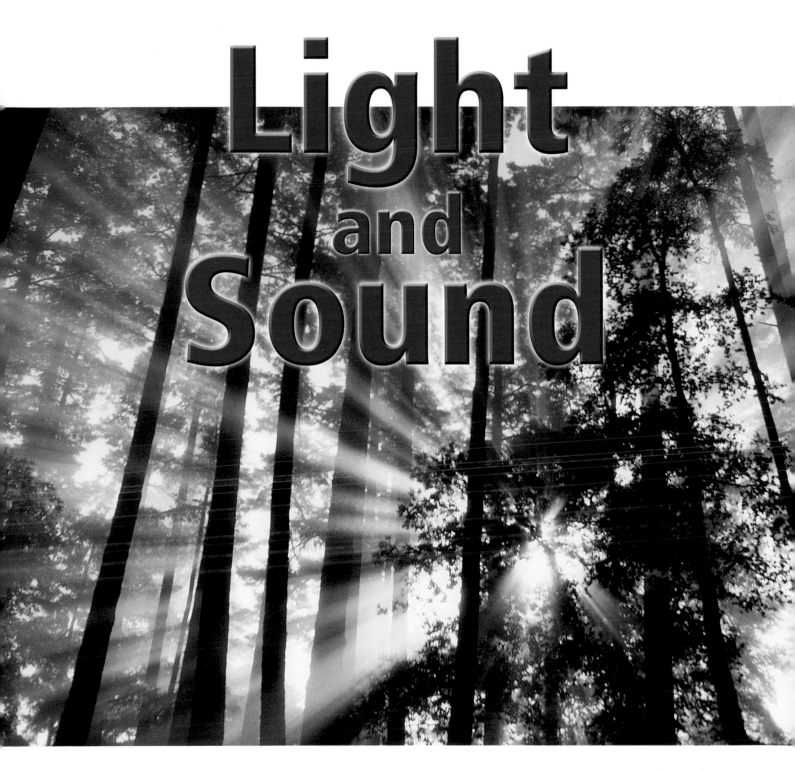

Visual Science Encyclopedia

Light and Sound

▲ Sunlight shining through redwoods in a morning fog in California. The picture is a good example of the way that light travels in straight lines.

How to use this book

Every word defined in this book can be found in alphabetical order on pages 3 to 47. There is also a full index on page 48. A number of other features will help you get the most out of the *Visual Science Encyclopedia*. They are shown below.

Here you will find the first word defined on any left-hand page.

Here you will find the last word defined on any right-hand page.

Each word is shown in bold so it is easy to find.

Each new letter of the alphabet is clearly marked to help you find the word you are looking for quicker.

Other words defined in the book are highlighted in bold.

Illustrations for some words complement the text and provide further information on a topic.

Plus, many entries point to related words of interest.

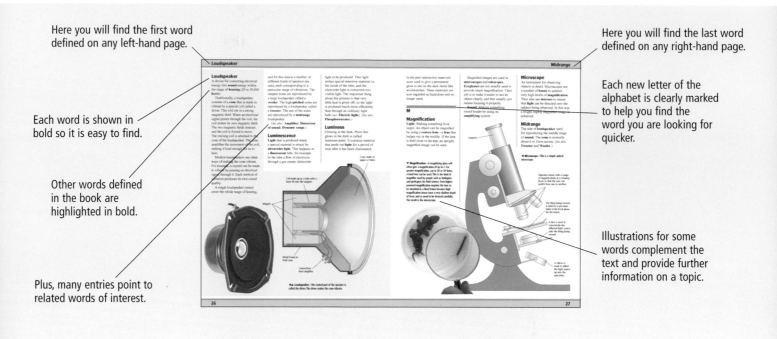

First published in 2002 by Atlantic Europe Publishing Company Ltd

Copyright © 2002 Atlantic Europe Publishing Company Ltd

Author
Brian Knapp, BSc, PhD

Art Director
Duncan McCrae, BSc

Senior Designer
Adele Humphries, BA, PGCE

Editors
Lisa Magloff, BA, and
Mary Sanders, BSc

Illustrations
David Woodroffe

Designed and produced by
EARTHSCAPE EDITIONS

Reproduced in Malaysia by
Global Colour

Printed in Hong Kong by
Wing King Tong Company Ltd.

Visual Science Encyclopedia
Volume 5 *Light and Sound*
A CIP record for this book is available from the British Library

ISBN 1-86214-029-4

Picture credits
All photographs are from the Earthscape Editions photolibrary except the following:
(c=centre t=top b=bottom l=left r=right)

NASA 5tr.

This product is manufactured from sustainable managed forests. For every tree cut down, at least one more is planted.

A

Aberration

A flaw in a **lens**. The lens does not produce an accurate, clear image. For example, if the lens is not the right shape, a straight line may appear curved when seen near the edge of the lens. If the line is curved towards the centre of the lens, the problem is called barrel distortion; if it is curved away from the centre, it is called pincushion distortion.

Absorption of light

The change of **light** striking an object into heat. As a result, the amount of light gradually lessens. If we shine a **beam of light** over a long distance, some of the light will be soaked up, or absorbed, by the water droplets and dust particles in the air. As a result, the light will appear fainter. It was partly to get around this problem that the Hubble **telescope** was sent into space. Hubble 'sees' many more faint objects than can be seen by telescopes on Earth because light from the objects is not absorbed by the atmosphere.

Some materials just absorb one kind of light. They are called filters. A red filter, for example, absorbs all lengths of light except red. Water absorbs red light, which is why sea water appears blue. The ice in an ice cave or a crevasse appears blue for the same reason. (*See also:* **Colour filters** and **Reflection**.)

Acoustics

The scientific study of **sound**. The word acoustics comes from the Greek word *akoustikos*, meaning related to **hearing**.

The word acoustics is also used more narrowly to mean the effect of objects or walls on music or speech. If a room contains a large amount of sound-absorbing material, such as curtains and carpets, the reflections of the sound are lessened, and the acoustics are

▼ **Absorption of light** – Ice and water absorb red light, so the sea and glacier ice appear blue.

described as 'dead'. If the room has hard, bare surfaces, such as in a church, sound is readily reflected and **echoes** become important. The acoustics of this type of room are called 'live'. (*See also:* **Anechoic chamber** and **Reverberation**.)

Afterglow

The glow that appears in the western sky just after sunset, and which can last for up to an hour. Even when the Sun has set as far as people on the ground are concerned, it has not set for people in a plane high above. **Sunlight** still reaches the upper sky long after the Sun has set on the ground. If the sunlight hits tiny particles of dust and ice in the upper air, some of the **light** can be reflected down to the ground, producing a glow. (A glow also appears before sunrise in the eastern sky for the same reason.)

Afterglows are most dramatic when the air has a lot of dust in it, for example, when it has not rained for a long time, and especially soon after a volcanic eruption, when the volcano has shot lots of dust high into the air.

▼ **Afterglow** – An evening afterglow.

Alto

From the Italian, meaning 'high'. It applies to singing. It is the vocal range above the tenor. Female alto voices (*see:* **Human voice**) are often called contralto.

Alto **musical instruments** such as the alto saxophone, alto clarinet and alto flute also have a high range of notes. (*See also:* **Bass**; **Tenor**; **Treble**.)

Amplifier

Converts a low-power signal from a pre-amplifier into the high-power signal (tens to hundreds of **watts**) needed to drive a **loudspeaker**.

Amplitude

The height of a wave (**light wave** or **sound wave**) as seen on a trace. It is a measure of the **brightness** of a source of **light** or the loudness of a **sound**.

This is a wave with a small amplitude.

This is a wave with a large amplitude.

▲ **Amplitude** – The height of a wave shows the amplitude.

Anechoic chamber

A room where the walls, ceiling and floor have been covered with **sound**-absorbing material to stop reflections. It has 'dead' **acoustics**. It is useful in testing equipment such as **loudspeakers** to find out their real characteristics.

Angle of incidence

The angle at which a **ray** of **light** approaches a **mirror** or transparent material, such as a block of glass.

Angle of reflection

The angle at which a **ray** of **light** leaves a **mirror**. It is always the same as the **angle of incidence**.

Angle of refraction

The angle at which a **ray** of **light** bends when it goes across the boundary between two transparent substances, such as air and glass. The ray is made steeper when it enters a denser substance such as water. (*See also:* **Refraction of light**.)

▼ **Angle of incidence/Angle of reflection** – When light rays arrive at a mirror, the angle of incidence is equal to the angle of reflection. Both are measured with respect to a line drawn at right angles to the mirror.

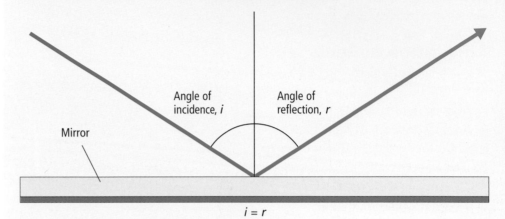

Angle of incidence, i

Angle of reflection, r

Mirror

$i = r$

▼ **Angle of refraction** – When light enters a transparent block or liquid, the light is bent downwards. The angle between the light ray and a line at right angles to the surface is the angle of refraction.

Angle of incidence

Glass block

Angle of refraction

Aperture

The amount of **light** allowed into a **camera** (*see:* **f-number**).

Aurora

A curtain of yellowish-green, white and red lights that appear to dance in the night sky close to the poles. The display is called the aurora borealis in the Northern Hemisphere and the aurora australis in the Southern Hemisphere. It can be seen from Alaska and from places of similar latitude in North America and from northern Scandinavia and Russia. Occasionally it extends further south, when people as far south as northern Scotland can see the effects. In the Southern Hemisphere the effect can only be seen in Antarctica.

Each part of the curtain is a coloured band, several hundred kilometres long and stretching in the same direction as the Earth's magnetic field. The bands keep appearing and disappearing within seconds.

The auroras occur as the solar wind (a flow of particles from the Sun outwards into space) is influenced by the Earth's magnetic field.

▲ **Aurora** – Coloured patterns produced as the Sun's solar wind blows through the Earth's magnetic field.

Beat

In music the basic rhythmic unit of a bar (for example, four beats to the bar).

In **sound** and **light** the shape of waves produced by combining two waves (*see:* **Light waves** and **Sound waves**). It can be heard using a piano by striking a white key and its neighbouring black key near the bass end of the keyboard. The combined notes appear to fade out and then get stronger in a kind of throbbing pattern. They are the beats.

Beats are used to tune **musical instruments**. When a **tuning fork** and a piano string are hit at the same time, but the piano string is slightly out of tune, beats will be heard. When the string is exactly in tune, no beats are heard. They then have identical **pitch**.

B

Bass

The lowest male voice (*see:* **Human voice**). The lowest-**pitched** member of the violin family is called a double bass. (*See also:* **Alto; Tenor; Treble.**)

Beam of light

Light rays that have been made to run parallel. That is normally done by using reflectors and **lenses**. The way a torch bulb focuses light into a beam is one example.

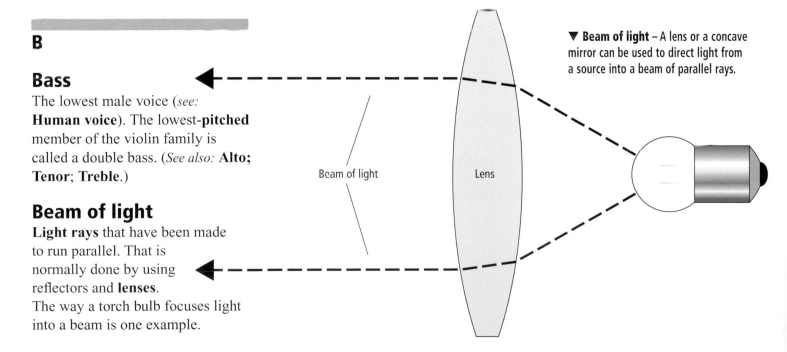

▼ **Beam of light** – A lens or a concave mirror can be used to direct light from a source into a beam of parallel rays.

Beam of light

Lens

Binoculars

The objective lens has a bulging shape to gather light. The bigger the objective lens, the better it is at light gathering. Light comes through the objective lens and is turned upside down and back to front. As it is bounced through the prisms, the light is turned so that we see an upright image again.

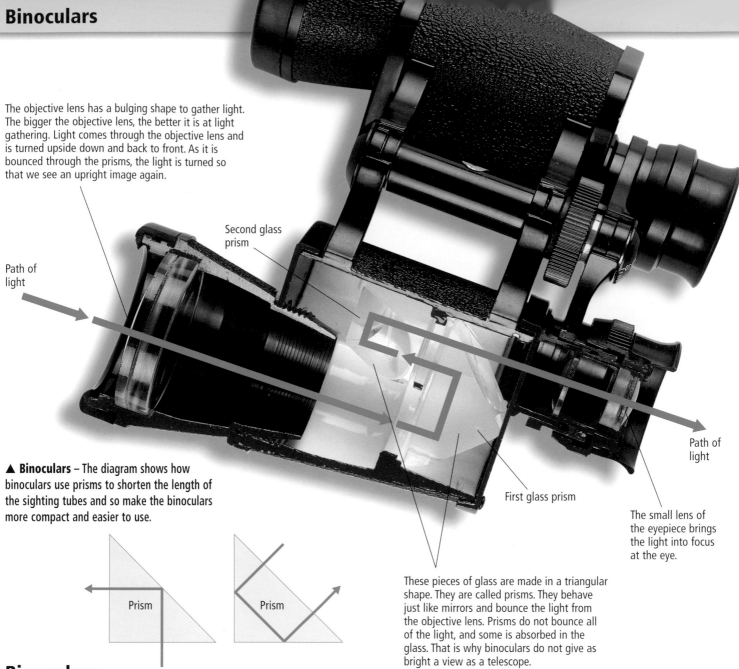

Second glass prism

Path of light

Path of light

First glass prism

▲ **Binoculars** – The diagram shows how binoculars use prisms to shorten the length of the sighting tubes and so make the binoculars more compact and easier to use.

Prism

Prism

These pieces of glass are made in a triangular shape. They are called prisms. They behave just like mirrors and bounce the light from the objective lens. Prisms do not bounce all of the light, and some is absorbed in the glass. That is why binoculars do not give as bright a view as a telescope.

The small lens of the eyepiece brings the light into focus at the eye.

Binoculars

Paired **telescopes** that use **prisms** to bend the **light** back on itself and so reduce the length of the sighting tube.

The key to this is to use a pair of prisms in each sighting tube. Each sighting tube is focused separately by rotating the eyepiece. The **focal length** of the sighting tubes is also adjustable using the knurled centre wheel.

Bioluminescence

The way in which some animals are able to create **light** by chemical reactions in the surface cells of their bodies. Fireflies and other insects are examples.

Brass

Any **wind instrument** in which the lips of the player are used to set up vibrations in the instrument (*see:* **Resonance**). The lips are placed against a cup-shaped mouthpiece and are used in the same way as a **reed**. Instruments like the trumpet are usually made of brass or other metal.

Brightness

The amount of **light** that a source appears to give out, or that is reflected from a surface. It is measured in **candelas**.

C

C

A symbol used in mathematical equations for the **speed of light** or the **speed of sound** (so you have to know which of them you are talking about). The most famous equation using the symbol is Einstein's theory of relativity, built around the equation:

$e = mc^2$ where

e = energy, m = mass and c = the speed of light.

Camera

A light-tight box containing a **lens** and film that is sensitive to **light**. When a shutter over the lens is opened, the light passes through the lens and reaches the film. The light alters special chemicals on the film. When the film is developed, the chemicals change. These changes can then be used to make a print or a transparency.

Cameras are now filled with gadgets to help photographers see the image through the lens, **focus** the lens properly, get the right amount of light on the film (the correct exposure) and wind the film. However, the principle that was demonstrated in the first pinhole camera remains the same.

The lens on a camera is the key to what kind of result you can get. On a 35mm camera a standard lens is called a 50mm lens. It gathers light from an angle of view 45° from the horizontal and gives the same sort of view as the human **eye**. It is the lens on most 35mm cameras when they are sold. By contrast, a telephoto lens gathers light from just 5°. Wide-angle lenses are those with **apertures** smaller than 50mm. An 8mm lens is called a fish-eye lens and it gathers light from 180°. New lenses, called zoom lenses, have a variable focus, allowing the photographer to change the angle that is captured. The smaller the angle captured, the greater the enlargement. (*See also:* **Colour filters**; **Depth of field**; **f-number**.)

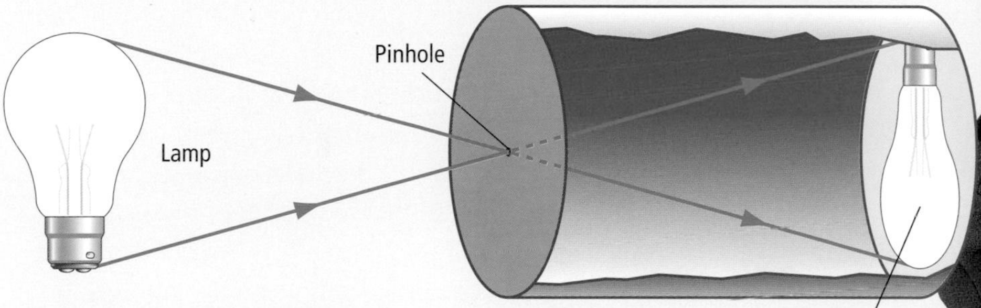

Pinhole

Lamp

Image projected onto translucent screen

▲▼► **Camera** – The simplest camera is a pinhole (top and top right). However, the small size of the hole means that very little light gets through to the screen. If the hole is made bigger (right), the image is brighter but blurred. To get a sharp, bright image (bottom left), a lens must be used. Normally, a piece of photographic film Is placed where the screen is located in the diagram.

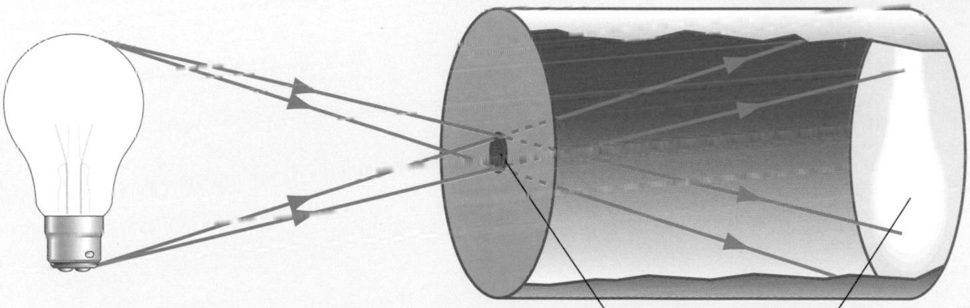

Larger pinhole produces a brighter but blurred image

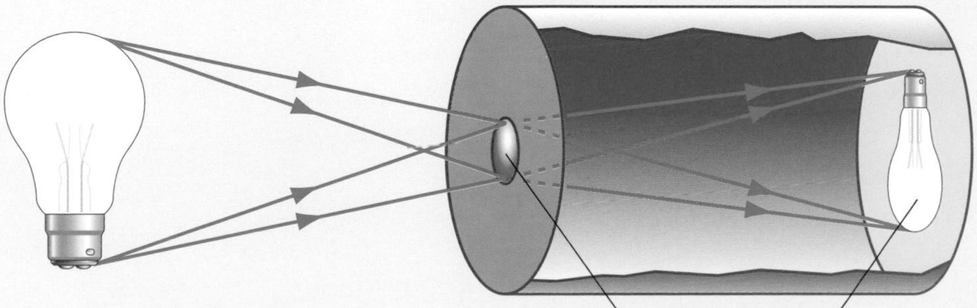

Lens produces sharp, bright image.

Camera with photographic film

Candela

A measure of **brightness**. Scientists first determined brightness by measuring the **light** given out by a 'standard candle'. That is how the term candela came to be used for brightness. Since then the candle itself has been replaced by more scientifically accurate measurements.

Candle power

The unit first used for measuring the **light** output of electric **lamps**. Before **electric light**, people used candles for **lighting**, and so they wanted a simple way of comparing electric lights to candles.

Colour

Light that reaches the **eye** and that does not appear **white**. Colour is very important and gives us much of the information our brain uses.

Not all animals see in colour. For example, dogs see in black and white. (*See also:* **Colour mixing**; **Colour vision**; **Hue**; **Saturation**.)

Colourants

Substances that are used to change the **colours** of something, such as **dyes** and **pigments**. They are used in paints.

Colour blindness

A condition in which some people cannot tell the difference between two kinds of coloured **light**, often red and green. It is thought that this problem lies in the brain rather than in the **eye**.

Such people do not see red or green, but only yellow, blue and grey. People with this problem still describe **colours** as red and green, but that is based on experience of what other people tell them.

Colour blindness is thought to be an inherited problem. It mainly affects men.

Colour filters

Sheets of glass or plastic that are designed to stop certain **light waves** from going through them. They are widely used in photography. For example, **ultraviolet** (UV) filters help prevent a photograph appearing too blue; a polaroid filter helps stop unwanted reflections from water, glass and metal. A blue filter is sometimes used for indoor photography with daylight film. It compensates for the fact that indoor light is redder than daylight. A red filter may help a black-and-white photographer get stronger sky tones. An orange filter will help a black-and-white photographer show red flowers against green leaves, while a green filter will make dark leaves appear lighter in tone.

Colour mixing

The **eye** can distinguish ten million **colours**. All colours are produced by mixing colours in one of two ways: by adding or by subtracting. To get colour mixtures by adding, new sources of **light** go in, for example, by adding **beams of light**. In subtracting, some light is taken away by using a filter.

Newton's colour circle shows how adding light beams of the same intensity can produce new colours. Adding **complementary colours** (those opposite each other in the circle) produce **white**. Other colours can be obtained by mixing coloured light beams. A mixture of red and yellow light produces orange, for example.

The basic, or **primary colours**, from which all other colours can be produced, are red, green and blue. When the three primary colours are added together in equal amounts, white is produced. Mixing colours by adding is what gives colours to the pictures shown on TV.

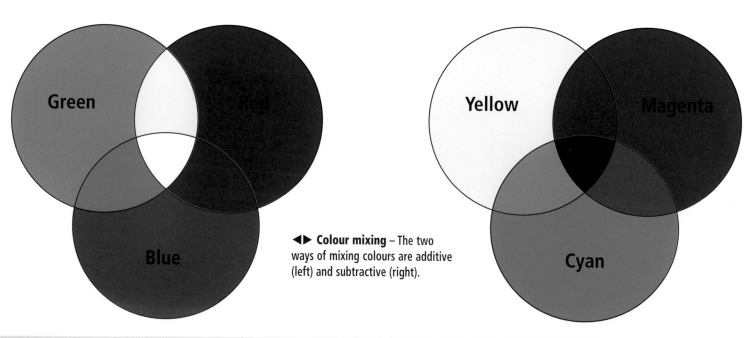

◀▶ **Colour mixing** – The two ways of mixing colours are additive (left) and subtractive (right).

Mixing colours for use on paper is the opposite of transmitting light. In this case the idea is to take certain colours out of **white light** so that only the desired colour is reflected from the surface. That is why mixing paints is called subtractive mixing. All paints, inks and **dyes** work in this way.

For example, mixing yellow and blue **pigments** causes the **absorption** of all colours but green.

The colours for subtraction are those that absorb red, green and blue light. They are blue–green (cyan), red–blue (magenta) and yellow. Confusion arises when some people call the primary colours used in paints red, yellow and blue (instead of magenta, yellow and cyan). For paints it is always best to think of the colours as red-absorbing, green-absorbing and blue-absorbing. Then you can see that **transmitted** and reflected light (*see:* **Reflection**) are part of the same system.

Colour of light sources

As objects, such as the filament in a light bulb, get hotter, the length of the **light waves** they give out changes. At a temperature of about 500°C the filament gives out a red light. As the temperature rises, the colour is yellow. Then, at about 5,000°C **white light** is given out.

A tungsten light bulb (*see:* **Electric light**) will reach about 3,000°C and give out a yellowish light. Average daylight from the Sun produces the same light at ground level as an object heated to 4,800°C; but from space the light from the Sun is whiter, appearing similar to the light from an object heated to 5,800°C.

Colour vision

To be able to see in **colour**, we must have detectors for colour inside our eyes. These detectors are found at the back of the eye. They are tiny groups of cells (called **cones**) that contain chemicals that are sensitive to different kinds of **light**. Although all cones are sensitive to every kind of light, it is thought that some cones are more sensitive to blue light, some more sensitive to green light and the rest more sensitive to red light.

Complementary colours

Colours that, when added together, produce **white**. Blues are complementary to yellows, reds to blue–greens and greens to red–purples. Newton's colour circle shows which colours are complementary and can be mixed to produce white. (*See also:* **Colour mixing** and **Primary colours**.)

Concave lens

A **lens** that curves inwards. These lenses cause **light rays** to spread apart, or diverge. They do not produce a **real image**, but a virtual (**imaginary**) image that appears to be in front of the lens. They are reducing lenses.

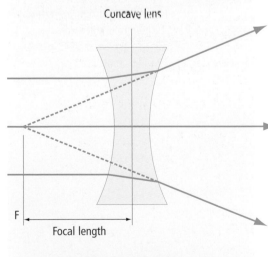

Concave lens

F
Focal length

▲ **Concave lens** – A concave lens produces a smaller virtual image that cannot be focused on a screen. It is used in eyeglasses for correcting the vision of people with myopia.

Concave mirror

▲▼ **Concave mirror** – A concave mirror makes things look bigger; the distortion depends on the amount that the lens is concave. A light placed at the centre of a concave mirror will be turned into a beam.

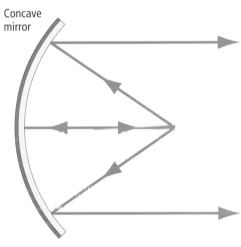

Concave mirror

Concave mirror

A **mirror** that curves inwards. **Light rays**, from a source such as a light bulb, travel outwards in all directions. Sometimes the light needs to be made into a **beam**, travelling in just one direction. A concave mirror is used to bounce the rays of light travelling away from where they are wanted and turn them into a beam travelling in just one direction. (*See also:* **Lighthouse**.)

Cone

The part of a **loudspeaker** that moves the air. Cones can be made of paper, plastics and newer materials such as Kevlar.

Cone also refers to the receptor cells in the eye that help us see in **colour** (*see:* **Colour vision** and **Vision**).

Contact lenses

Thin **lenses** worn on the surface of the **eye** to correct for defects of **vision**. The first contact lens was made by Adolf Fick in 1887. The modern contact lens, developed by Kevin Tuohy in 1948, is made of hard or soft plastic. It is held against the eye by the fluid that naturally covers the eye. A contact lens covers only the **iris** and the pupil.

Contact lenses can work better than **eyeglasses** in correcting some sight problems. However, many people prefer them for cosmetic reasons.

Converging lens

The name for a **convex lens**.

Convex lens

A **lens** that bulges at the centre. Convex lens are the most common kind of lenses, used in **eyeglasses**, **telescopes** and **microscopes**. The human **eye** contains a convex lens. (*See also:* **Cornea**; **Magnification**; **Real image**.)

Convex mirror

A **mirror** that bulges out in the centre. Convex mirrors give a much wider angle of view than flat mirrors. They are used in car mirrors and in security mirrors in stores. They tend to make

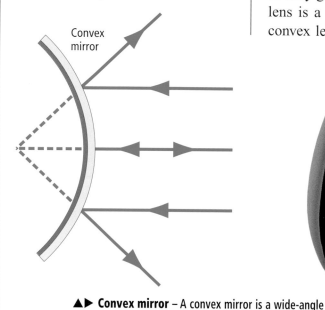

Convex mirror

▲▶ **Convex mirror** – A convex mirror is a wide-angle mirror, enabling a wide angle of view. It is used as security mirrors and in some car wing mirrors. It makes objects look smaller and further away than they really are.

▼ **Convex lens** – A convex lens produces a real image. It is a magnifying lens, used for magnifying glasses, camera lenses, projectors and so on. It is also the most common form of eyeglass, used for people who have difficulty focusing on objects close to them.

objects look further away than they really are.

Cornea

The front part of the outer surface of the **eye**. It acts like a **convex lens**. The cornea is the place where **light rays** are bent and brought into the eye. It is a fixed lens. The part of the eye called the lens is an adjustable fine tuner for the light already gathered by the cornea. The lens is a double convex lens.

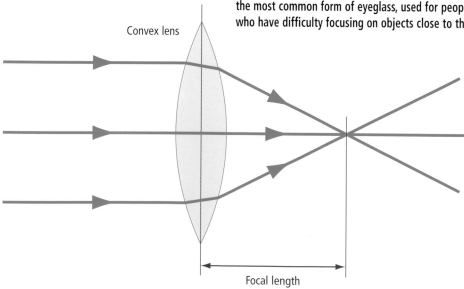

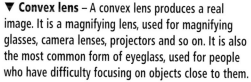

Convex lens

Focal length

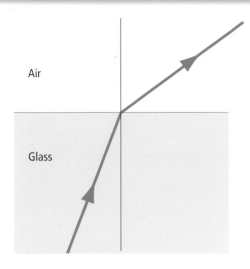

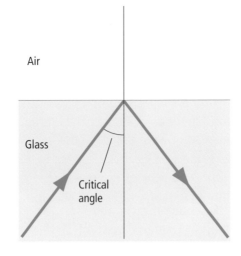

Critical angle

Short for the critical angle of total internal reflection. It is the angle at which a transparent material stops allowing **light** to pass through it and begins to reflect it instead. To understand this, imagine looking directly at a sheet of glass. It will be completely transparent. Now turn the glass. At a certain angle you will no longer be able to see through it, but the glass will behave like a **mirror** instead. That is the critical angle.

▲ **Critical angle** – Light passing through a glass block will go back out into the air unless it strikes at a wide angle. Then it will be reflected. The critical angle is the maximum angle for refraction.

D

Damping

Making a vibration smaller in order to stop **reverberation** and act as **soundproofing**. (*See also:* **Decay**.)

Decibel

A scale developed to describe the intensity (power) of **sound**.

The decibel scale is similar to the Richter scale used for earthquakes and is designed to take in a huge range of energy levels. The term 'bel' is taken from the name of Alexander Graham Bell, inventor of the telephone. A decibel (dB) is one-tenth of a bel.

On the decibel scale the smallest sound that can be heard is 0dB. Sound becomes painful (because the pressure on the **ear** is too great) at about 135dB. Each 3dB increase in sound represents a doubling of sound intensity. (*See also:* **Sound level**.)

Decay

The gradual reduction in the size of a **sound wave** so that the **sound** fades away and finally stops. Decay can be speeded up by using **damping**. In many **musical instruments** decay is slow, allowing the instrument to give the full range of its sound. (*See also:* **Reverberation**.)

Depth of field

The range of distances over which a photograph will be sharp, or in **focus**. The depth of field depends on how close the **camera** is to the object, the type of **lens** and the size of the **aperture** used. In general, the wider the angle of the lens, the smaller the aperture (**f-number**). The farther away the scene, the greater the depth of field. A 50mm lens on a 35mm camera set to focus on 10m will have a depth of field from about 4 metres to infinity.

▶ **Depth of field** – The depth of field depends on the focal length of the lens and the aperture. If the aperture is large, the depth of field is smaller. In the left-hand picture the focus is on the house – the flowers in the foreground are out of focus because the depth of field doesn't reach that close. In the right-hand picture the focus is on the flowers, and the house is out of focus.

Diffraction of light

The bending of **light** when it passes around the edge of an object rather than through it (which is called **refraction**). The effect was first described in 1818 by the French physicist Augustin-Jean Fresnel. It happens where the **wavelength** of the light is large in comparison with the object. The wave front bends around the object, and there is no **shadow**. To study this effect, a bright light is shone through glass etched with thousands of parallel lines per centimetre.

Diffraction of sound

The bending of **sound waves** around an object that occurs when the waves are long compared with the size of the object. Because sound waves have long **wavelengths** – often more than a metre – **sound** commonly curves around objects. That is why you can hear a person speaking from the other side of a tree, or why you can hear around the corner of a building.

Only large objects – like mountains – will block and reflect sound waves.

Dispersion of light

The separation of **white light** into its **rainbow** of **colours**. This property was first used by Sir Isaac Newton to show that white light is a mixture of colours.

Distortion of sound

Distortion occurs when the **tones** that were present in the original **sound** are not faithfully reproduced by the **loudspeaker**, or new tones are added that did not exist in the original sound. Distortion often occurs because the material of the loudspeaker **cone** is not flexible enough, or because the coil in the base of the loudspeaker is not sufficiently free to move.

Diverging lens

(*See:* **Concave lens**.)

Dome

A dome-shaped part of a **loudspeaker**. A dome can be used instead of a **cone**. It is found in some smaller loudspeakers. A dome can be made from paper, fabric, thin aluminium or titanium.

Doppler effect of light

A shift in **wavelength** that occurs when **light** arrives from a source that is travelling very fast towards or away from the observer. The Doppler effect of light does not affect our everyday experience and is really only of concern to astronomers. They can use the Doppler effect to find out how fast objects in space are travelling. A source moving away from the observer very fast is seen as a redder light than usual. That is called the red shift. It has been used as evidence for suggesting that the universe is expanding, because all stars show a red shift, so they must all be travelling away from us very fast.

Doppler effect of sound

A change in **pitch** caused by a **sound** source moving towards or away from an observer. The pitch is higher when the source and observer are getting closer and lower when they are moving apart. You hear the Doppler shift when a fast-moving train or vehicle approaches and then passes.

For example, if a racing car is moving towards the listener, more **sound waves** enter the listener's **ear** each second than the car engine produces. The sound seems higher pitched to the listener than it does to the driver.

When the racing car is moving away from the listener, fewer sound waves enter the listener's ear each second than the car engine produces. The sound now seems lower to the listener than it does to the driver. This explains the familiar 'eeeeoooowwwwww' sound as the car passes.

Dropout

A term used by **hi-fi** enthusiasts for a very weak response in part of a **loudspeaker** or **amplifier** range. If the sound system has a very noticeable dropout, it can spoil listening pleasure.

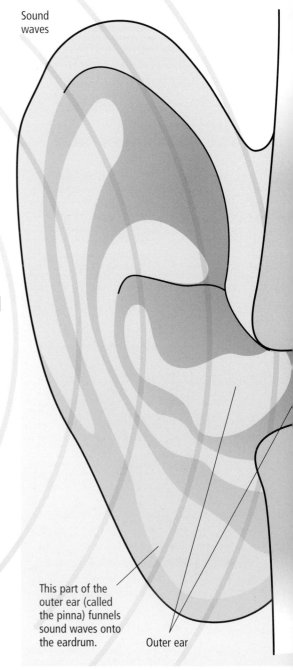

Sound waves

This part of the outer ear (called the pinna) funnels sound waves onto the eardrum.

Outer ear

Dye

A substance that has an intense **colour** and is used to tint materials (*See:* **Colourant**).

When a material is dyed, dye molecules come out of the dyeing solution and attach themselves onto the material to be dyed in such a way that they cannot be removed. The chemical used to help fix the dye is called a mordant. The mordant is put onto the material before the dye. When the dye is applied, the coloured chemicals in the dye combine with the mordant to fix the colour permanently.

Most modern, commercial dyes are made from crude oil.

Dynamic range

The **frequency** range over which the **ear** can hear, or a **loudspeaker** can produce **sound**. The dynamic range of the ear is greater than any speaker system can match. (*See also:* **Sound level**.)

E

Ear

The body's sound receiver. One of the most sensitive organs of the body, it is able to hear **sounds** that range over 10 octaves (15Hz to 20,000Hz) (*see:* **Hearing**) and sound intensities over a range of 1,000 billion to one. When the ear detects the faintest possible sound, it moves just a billionth of a centimetre. The ear can also detect a **frequency** difference of only a few cycles per second.

Two ears allow us to detect the direction the sound is coming from. The brain is able to sort out the many different sounds we hear in, say, a noisy street and focus on just one of them.

The ear and brain are able to pick out each new **sound wave** that reaches it and ignore the **echoes**. That makes it possible to understand speech in a room with **reverberation** (most rooms).

The ear is made of three parts: the outer ear, the middle ear and the inner ear. The outer ear consists of the part of the ear you can see, as far as the ear-drum. The middle ear reaches from the space behind the ear-drum to another, thin kind of ear-drum, called the aperture. The inner ear is a curled tube containing many fine hairs that detect the sound waves and change them into electrical signals. There are about 30,000 sound-detecting hairs and they all combine into one 'cable' that is less than a millimetre across. This cable goes directly to the brain.

When sound reaches the ear, it is channelled down to the ear-drum, which makes the ear-drum vibrate. On the other side of the ear-drum are three small bones that transfer the vibration to the aperture at the end of the inner ear. The inner ear is filled with a fluid. As the aperture vibrates, it sets the fluid in motion, and this sets the hairs of the inner ear into motion. Movements of the hairs then create the electrical signals that go to the brain. The hairs are of different lengths, so they vibrate at different frequencies. That is how we can tell one **pitch** from another.

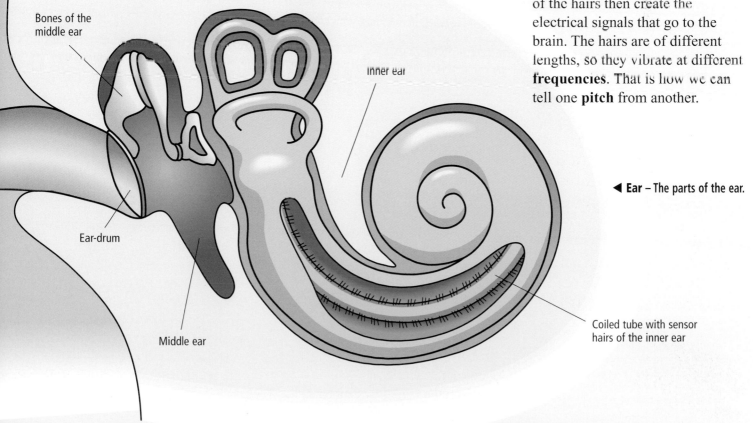

Bones of the middle ear

Ear-drum

Middle ear

Inner ear

◄ **Ear** – The parts of the ear.

Coiled tube with sensor hairs of the inner ear

Echo

A **sound** that reaches listeners more than 0.05 seconds after an initial sound has reached them directly. (*See also:* **Reverberation**.)

Electric light

Light produced when electrical energy is converted into **light energy**. This can be done using a spark (as in lightning or an arc **lamp**), by heating a filament (as in an ordinary **incandescent electric light** bulb), or by making special chemicals glow (as in a fluorescent tube).

Halogen light

▶ **Electric light** – We use many forms of electric light, including the light from hot filaments: incandescent, halogen lights, the light from the reaction of charged gases with phosphors – fluorescent lights – and the glowing of gases when an electric charge passes through them (neon lights, mercury vapour lights, sodium lights, and so on).

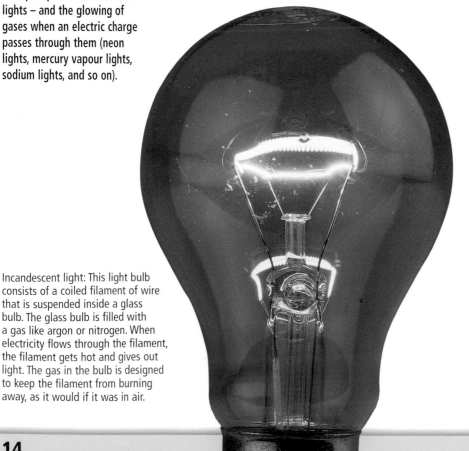

Incandescent light: This light bulb consists of a coiled filament of wire that is suspended inside a glass bulb. The glass bulb is filled with a gas like argon or nitrogen. When electricity flows through the filament, the filament gets hot and gives out light. The gas in the bulb is designed to keep the filament from burning away, as it would if it was in air.

Eye, eyesight

The organ that collects **light** and converts it into electrical signals that are then sent to the brain. The eyesight of all living things works in basically the same way. The eyes contain special cells that are sensitive to light and nerves that connect these cells directly to the brain.

The simplest 'eyesight' is found in some worms. They have light-sensitive cells on parts of their skins. Insects have lots of small eyes that cannot change their **focus**. They are called compound eyes. More developed animals have eyes that can focus light and alter the amount of it reaching the eye. In advanced animals the back of the eye may have millions of light-sensitive cells. Cells near the centre of the eye are cone-shaped (**cones**), while those near the edge are rod-shaped (rods).

The human eye is contained in an outer protective coat. The front of this coating is transparent and is called the **cornea**. On the inside at the back are the light-sensitive cells. This region is called the **retina**.

Light passing through the cornea travels through the pupil of the eye, which changes size depending on the amount of light. It then passes through the **lens** and travels through the fluid inside the eye before reaching the retina.

The cornea, lens and liquid all have the same light-bending powers, so light does not get bent or distorted as it passes from one to another. Most of the light-bending happens at the outside of the cornea, while only fine-tuning and focusing of the light are done by the lens.

To work properly, the cornea has to be kept moist, which is why we have tear ducts and why we blink often.

The lens is made of elastic, transparent fibres. Over time these fibres become less elastic, and it becomes harder for the eye to focus. This usually causes problems focusing on objects that are close to the eye.

The **iris** is a thin, circular disc with a hole in the centre called the pupil. The iris contains a layer of coloured cells. They give the eye its

▼ **Eye, eyesight** – Many problems can occur with our eyesight. Some are shown here.

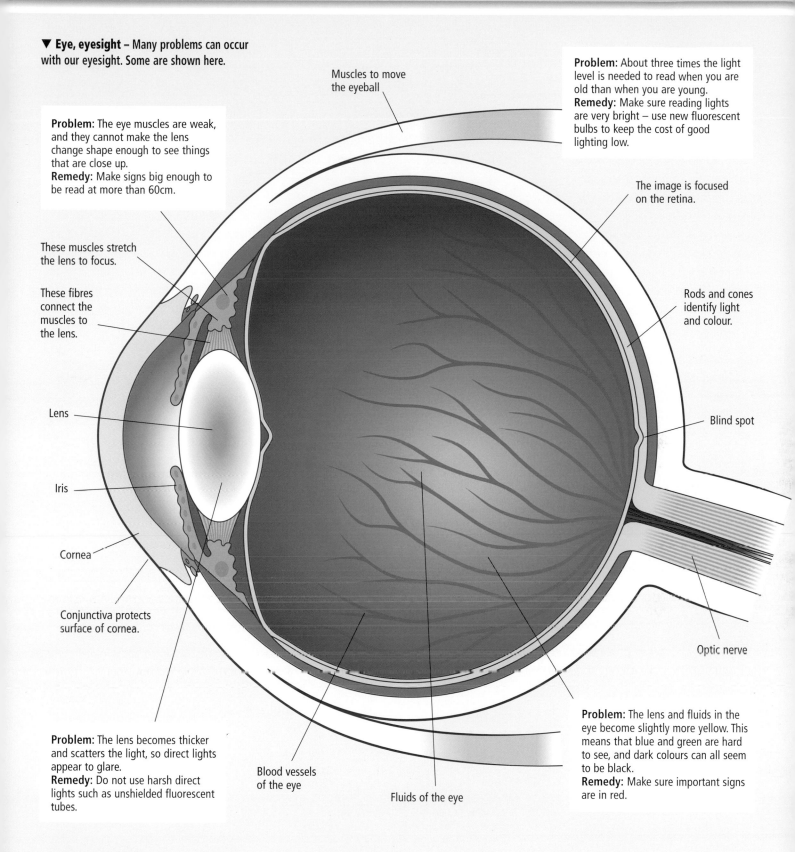

Muscles to move the eyeball

Problem: The eye muscles are weak, and they cannot make the lens change shape enough to see things that are close up.
Remedy: Make signs big enough to be read at more than 60cm.

Problem: About three times the light level is needed to read when you are old than when you are young.
Remedy: Make sure reading lights are very bright – use new fluorescent bulbs to keep the cost of good lighting low.

The image is focused on the retina.

These muscles stretch the lens to focus.

These fibres connect the muscles to the lens.

Rods and cones identify light and colour.

Lens

Iris

Blind spot

Cornea

Conjunctiva protects surface of cornea.

Optic nerve

Problem: The lens becomes thicker and scatters the light, so direct lights appear to glare.
Remedy: Do not use harsh direct lights such as unshielded fluorescent tubes.

Blood vessels of the eye

Fluids of the eye

Problem: The lens and fluids in the eye become slightly more yellow. This means that blue and green are hard to see, and dark colours can all seem to be black.
Remedy: Make sure important signs are in red.

colour. Brown eyes have a thick iris with lots of coloured cells; blue and grey eyes have a thin iris with less coloured cells.

The pupil changes size to allow just enough light into the retina. Too much light can damage the

sensitive cells in the retina. That is the reason we must never look at very bright light sources, such as the Sun.

The human eye is designed to see through air. That is why it is so difficult to see under water. Water

and the tissues of the eye are very similar, so the eye does not bend the light as much in water as in air. That is why you need a face mask to see properly under water.

Eyeglasses

Also called just 'glasses', or spectacles, eyeglasses are **lenses** mounted in a frame designed to rest in front of the eyes and correct problems with **vision**. The use of eyeglasses began in China and Europe in ancient times. At first, natural crystals of quartz were used, then curved glass. Eyeglasses improved with the knowledge of how lenses worked and with better technology for casting curved glass and polishing it to the required shape. Places like Venice, in Italy, and Nuremberg, in Germany, that were originally famous for their glassware later became known for their eyeglasses.

The first glasses used bulging (**convex**) lenses and corrected for long-sightedness. It was only in the 16th century that dished (**concave**) lenses were developed for shortsightedness (myopia).

In 1784 Benjamin Franklin invented bifocals, making the upper part of the lens suitable for use when looking in the distance and the lower part useful for reading.

Modern lenses begin as a sheet of plate glass and are then shaped by using fine abrasive powder and specially shaped tools. Many lenses are now made of plastic. Since plastic is less dense than glass, plastic eyeglasses are not as heavy. Plastic scratches more easily than glass, but it is less brittle than glass and less likely to shatter.

Contact lenses are small lenses held on the surface of the **eye**. They are made from either glass or plastic.

Sunglasses often contain no corrective lenses at all and are simply coated with material that reduces the **light** passing through the lens. Tinted coating can also be applied to prescription glasses.

F

Fibre optics

A way of sending **light** over long distances through transparent fibres. The fibres can be glass or plastic. It does not matter whether the fibres are straight or curved.

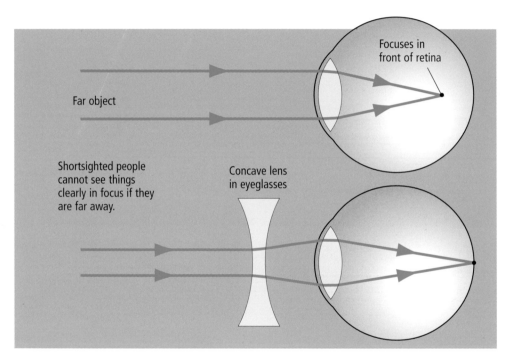

Far object

Focuses in front of retina

Shortsighted people cannot see things clearly in focus if they are far away.

Concave lens in eyeglasses

▲ **Eyeglasses** – A concave lens is used for people who cannot see things in focus when they are at a distance. In this case the lens of the eye brings light to a focus in front of the back of the eye. The glass lens slightly diverges the light, so that the eye lens can then bring objects to a focus on the back of the eye.

▶ **Eyeglasses** – A convex lens is used for people who cannot see things in focus when they are very close. This is the more usual eye problem. In this case the lens of the eye brings light to a focus behind the back of the eye. The glass lens slightly converges the light, so that the eye lens can then bring objects to a focus on the back of the eye.

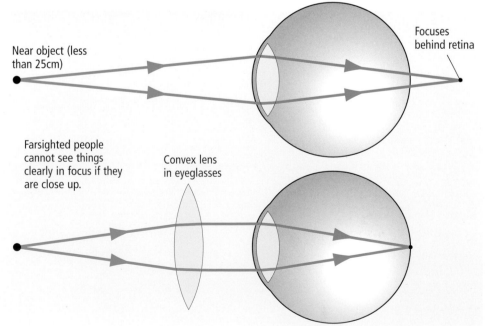

Near object (less than 25cm)

Focuses behind retina

Farsighted people cannot see things clearly in focus if they are close up.

Convex lens in eyeglasses

The reason why light moves down the fibre and does not come out of it depends on the properties of the glass or plastic. Light travelling down the fibre strikes the edge of the fibre with a glancing angle and so is continually reflected back inside the fibre. The light never approaches the edge of the fibre at a sharp enough angle to get out (*see:* **Critical angle**). The light moves down the fibre by bouncing, or ricocheting, off the fibre walls.

All fibres are coated in a protective glass or plastic. A glass-coated fibre is made by placing a rod inside a glass tube and then heating and drawing out the rod and the tube. They form very fine fibres.

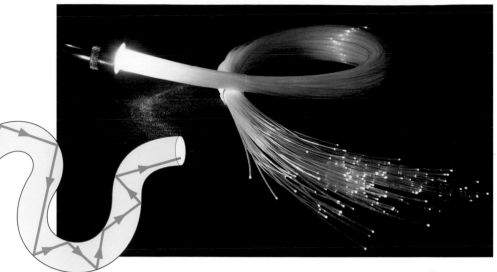

Fluorescence

Taking in invisible waves and changing them so that they become visible. The coating on a fluorescent tube does this, as do the tiny spots of material that cover the inside of a television tube.

The materials that do this are called phosphors. (*See also:* **Luminescence**; **Phosphorescence**.)

f-number (f-stop)

Camera lenses often have f-numbers around the rim. The numbers are related to the amount of **light** that goes through the lens. The 'f' in this case stands for 'fraction'. Each f-number is the fraction of the **focal length** of the lens. Typical numbers are f/2.8, f/4, f/5.6, f/8, f/11 and f/16. In this sequence each higher number indicates a smaller **lens** opening that allows only half as much light to pass than the number immediately smaller than it. A camera set at f8 only allows in half as much light as a camera set at f5.6. (*See also:* **Aperture**.)

▲ **Fibre optics** – A glass fibre keeps light inside because the light always strikes the side of the glass at more than the critical angle and is always reflected back inside the glass.

Focus, focal length, focal plane

The point at which **rays** of **light** converge, having passed through a **lens** or been reflected from a **mirror**.

The focal length is the distance from the lens to the point at which rays of light from a long way away come together (converge) to a point. The focal length depends on the degree of curving of the mirror and the type of glass or plastic used to make the lens.

Lenses of longer focal length gather light from a smaller angle than those with a small focal length. Such lenses, when used on **cameras**, are called telephoto lenses. Lenses with a small focal length are called wide-angle lenses.

The focal plane is the upright plane running through the focal point. An image of an object on it will be clear but inverted (upside down and back to front). Light from close-up objects comes together at a point behind the focal plane and will not be in focus. That is the reason why the position of the lens has to be changed (i.e. focused) in a camera depending on the distance away of the object that needs to be in focus.

▼ **Focus** – The focus of a lens is the place where parallel rays of light, from a source a long distance away, come together. The focal plane runs through this point.

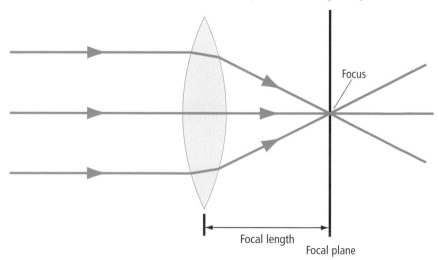

Focus

Focal length

Focal plane

In a high-frequency wave the crests and troughs are close together.

In a low-frequency wave the crests and troughs are spread apart.

▲ **Frequency** – The frequency is the number of cycles of a wave per second. On a wave trace it is seen as a larger number of complete wave cycles. The diagram on the right is a low-frequency wave – it has few complete cycles. The diagram on the left is a high-frequency wave – it has many cycles.

Frequency

The number of times an object moves backwards and forwards per second. This back and forth movement is called an oscillation.

Each complete oscillation produces one **sound wave**. The number of sound waves passing a given point each second is the frequency of that **sound**.

Frequency is measured in **hertz (Hz)** or kilohertz (kHz) meaning thousands of Hz. A 1,000Hz (1kHz) **tone** moves your eardrum back and forth 1,000 times each second. (*See also:* **Dynamic range** and **Pitch**.)

Fresnel lens

A **lens** made out of a series of rings, one inside the other. Each ring is a lens. The purpose of this arrangement is to concentrate the **light** into a narrow **beam** for use with **lighthouses**, searchlights and floodlights. The Fresnel lens is quite lightweight – an ordinary lens that could do the same job would be immensely heavy. Fresnel lenses can also be found on traffic signals.

Fresnel lenses are made of plastic as well as glass. They are very thin and are used in some **cameras**. They help increase the **brightness** on the outer part of the

viewing screen.

The idea of ring lenses was developed by Georges-Louis Leclerc de Buffon in 1748, but its use in lighthouse lenses by Augustin-Jean Fresnel meant that eventually the lens became associated with lighthouses and thus became known as a Fresnel lens.

Fundamental

The lowest **tone** of a musical note. The fundamental is also called the first **harmonic**. (*See also:* **Overtones**.)

G

Glasses

(*See:* **Eyeglasses**.)

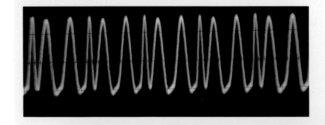

H

Harmonic

A **tone** whose **frequency** is an exact multiple of the frequency of the **fundamental** (lowest) tone. A harmonic is one kind of **overtone**.

When a note is played together with its harmonics, the fundamental tone is called the first harmonic. The overtone that is produced by a vibration exactly double the fundamental is called the second harmonic; the tone produced by a vibration exactly three times the fundamental is called the third harmonic and so on.

▼ **Harmonic** – These are some of the harmonics of the note C.

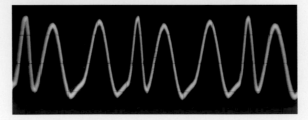

The wave pattern of an oboe playing a top C (a high-frequency note)

The wave pattern of an oboe playing a middle C (a medium-frequency note)

The wave pattern of an oboe playing a bottom C (a low-frequency note)

Every note played on a **musical instrument** consists of a fundamental tone plus many harmonics. It is called a musical tone.

Hearing

The capture of **sound** by a sensitive part of the skin (in the case of humans by the **ear**). All arthropods (insects, spiders, crabs and so on) and vertebrates (mammals, fish and so on) can hear, although they each have a different hearing range and hear best in different mediums. For example, humans hear best in air, while fish hear best in water.

Some living things, such as insects, spiders and fish, can sense the speed of the vibration. Most others sense sound by the pressure of the sound on a sensitive piece of skin (in the case of humans the ear-drum).

Insects mainly hear through sensitive regions on the middle part (thorax) of their bodies. Mosquitoes hear through their antennae; cockroaches and similar insects hear through their abdomen in the range of 100 to 3,000Hz.

Insects may have one or two places that are sensitive to sound. All vertebrates have two ears, which enable them to sense not only the nature of the sound but also its direction. Bats use an **echo-**locating system, sending out high-**frequency sound waves** and then listening to the reflected waves to judge the position of objects in their path.

The ears of mammals are more complex than in other vertebrates and include an outer ear, which acts like a funnel, collecting sound and feeding it down to the ear-drum. Humans can hear sounds at frequencies ranging from 15Hz to 15,000Hz, and children can hear sounds as high as 20,000Hz.

Sounds below 15Hz are called infrasound, and those higher than 20,000Hz are called **ultrasound**. Humans cannot hear them, but some birds, bats and insects use ultrasound. Dogs can also hear ultrasound and dog whistles normally use ultrasound. Dog whistles are normally also given an audible whistle, otherwise the owners do not know the whistle is working.

Hertz (Hz)

The unit of **frequency**. It is equal to the number of wave crests that pass a fixed point each second. The number of hertz is therefore equal to the number of complete wave cycles per second. In **sound** the larger the number of hertz, the higher the sound. In **light**, **colours** closer to the red end of the **spectrum** have a larger number of hertz.

The unit is named after the 19th-century German physicist Heinrich Hertz.

Hi-fi

Short for high-fidelity, meaning good-quality **sound**. To be hi-fi, equipment must be able to cover 20 to 20,000Hz, and preferably 15 to 20,000Hz. The lowest notes on organs and pianos are 16.4 and 24.5Hz respectively. (*See also:* **Dropout**.)

Hue

The 'colour' property of a **colour**, such as red, yellow, green or blue.

Human voice

Humans make **sounds** by using air escaping from their lungs. The sounds we make are produced in a variety of ways. For example, vowels are produced when the vocal chords chop the air stream from the lungs into short bursts of air. The rate of chopping controls the **pitch** of the voice. It is as low as 100 pulses per second for males, 200 pulses per second for females, and more for children.

The windpipe amplifies the voice. While the vocal chords act like a **reed**, the windpipe acts like a pipe, giving the sound its quality and amplification.

The sounds of speech are controlled by the way we hold our tongue, lips and palate.

Some sounds, such as the consonants b, d, f and others, do not involve the vocal chords; the sound is simply the air being blown from the lungs, combined with the movement of tongue, lips and palate. With other speech sounds, such as n, the air is allowed to come out of the nose. (*See also:* **Alto**; **Bass**; **Tenor**; **Treble**.)

I

Imaginary image

The image that you see when you look into a **mirror** or through **eyeglasses**. This image cannot be seen on a screen or made into a photograph. The term virtual image is also used. An imaginary image is produced when you are close to a **lens** (*see:* **Concave lens**). The image is always upright. That is why we can see an enlarged upright image through eyeglasses.

Incandescence, incandescent light

The **light** produced when something glows. The effect is most commonly used in an ordinary light bulb, which are formally called incandescent light bulbs (*see:* **Electric light**). Electricity flowing through the filament makes the filament glow, or incandesce, white hot.

Index of refraction

Light does not travel at the same **speed** in all materials. In space light travels at 300,000 kilometres per second. In glass it travels only two-thirds as fast. The refractive index is a term used to describe the power of a material to slow light compared to space (a vacuum). The refractive index of glass is about 1.5, and the refractive index of water is about 1.3.

Infrared light

Light that is just beyond our **vision**. The longest waves we can see belong to red light. Waves slightly longer than that are called infrared waves. Some animals, especially insects, can see infrared waves. William Herschel, a German-born British astronomer, discovered infrared radiation by using a thermometer to look at the heat produced by light passed through a **prism** (a glass wedge). He found that the thermometer increased in temperature when he placed it just outside the red part of the **rainbow**.

Interference

The pattern of light and dark bands that are produced when two or more **light waves** cross. The principle can be imagined by comparing light waves to two pebbles dropped into a pond. In some places where the waves cross, they add and make a higher wave, while in other places they subtract and make a lower wave. In light places of adding produce stronger, or brighter, light, while places of subtraction make less light. This pattern is at its simplest with light beams of a single colour. When interference occurs in **white light**, the pattern can be more complex. The coloured patterns on oil, soap bubbles, butterfly and bird wings,

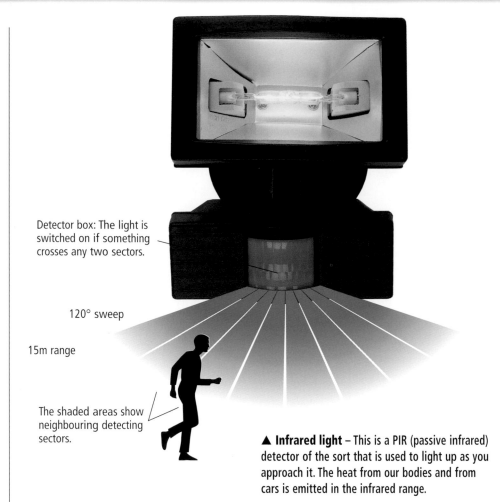

Detector box: The light is switched on if something crosses any two sectors.

120° sweep

15m range

The shaded areas show neighbouring detecting sectors.

▲ **Infrared light** – This is a PIR (passive infrared) detector of the sort that is used to light up as you approach it. The heat from our bodies and from cars is emitted in the infrared range.

and some beetles are the result of interference with white light. In these cases interference occurs because light is reflected from both the upper and lower surfaces of thin sheets of transparent material.

Iris

Two sheets of muscle between the front of the **eye** (the **cornea**) and the **lens**. They have coloured cells that give the eye its **colour**. In the centre is a hole called the pupil. The size of the pupil is changed to let in more or less **light** as the iris muscles contract or expand.

L

Lamp

A device that burns fuel to produce **light**.

The earliest lamps used oil. A wick was placed in a dish of oil and ignited. The wick burned with a yellow flame until the oil was used up.

Gas lamps burned a mixture of air and coal gas.

Arc lamps rely on a giant spark occurring between two electrically charged rods. That produces a very bright **white light**.

Gradually, all these forms of lamp were replaced in general use by the electric lamp. The most common form of **electric light** is a bulb that contains a filament of tungsten metal. When electricity passes through the filament, it glows brightly. It is called an **incandescent** lamp.

Laser

A device that produces an intense **beam of light** of a single **colour**. The word laser stands for 'light amplification by stimulated emission of radiation'.

In a laser **light** of a certain colour is shone onto a crystal. It makes the crystal send out more light of exactly the same colour. If this process is repeated, a very powerful beam of light is produced. The first laser was built in 1960 by Theodore H. Maiman of the United States, using a rod of ruby.

LED

Light-emitting diode. When electricity passes through a special kind of semi-conductor called a diode, the material gives out **light**. The light given out can be quite powerful. LEDs also have a far longer life than ordinary bulbs. Most indicator lights on electrical equipment are LEDs, while the central brake lights on the rear of new cars are also made from a row of LEDs.

Lens

A piece of transparent glass, plastic, or crystal that has one or both sides curved in such a way as to bend the **light** to make an image. **Eyes** also contain lenses, but they are flexible and made from flexible fibres. In this way eyes are adjustable lenses.

Lenses are used in **cameras**, **microscopes**, projectors and **telescopes**, as well as **eyeglasses** and **contact lenses**.

You can also see lenses at work in the natural world. A raindrop on a leaf or stem will act as a natural enlarger, **magnifying** the surface it is on. A glass bowl or drinking glass filled with water will bend light and bring it to a point, or **focus**.

People began to use lenses to help with **eyesight** in the 13th century. The word lens comes from the rounded shape of the lens, which people thought looked like a lentil (*lens* in Latin).

The first telescopes were made by lens-makers. Galileo built a telescope of his own in about 1609, using two lenses. At about the same time people began to build microscopes, again using two lenses.

By the 18th century the first lenses were being made that did not produce undesirable **colour** problems (*see:* **Aberration**). They were complex lenses – two or more lenses stuck together to produce better quality.

In 1866 the German optician Ernst Abbe, who worked for Carl Zeiss in Jena, stated the

▼ **Lens** – The way curved transparent materials bend the light to bring it to a focus can be shown by this simple demonstration. A number of slits are cut in a piece of paper, and a drinking glass placed in front of them. The rays of light not blocked by the glass continue as parallel beams, while those that go through the glass are brought to a focus. Any curved glass or other transparent object will focus rays in this way, but to be useful, the curved glass needs to be designed with a certain focal length. It is then called a lens.

Light source such as flashlight

Teeth cut in card (or comb) used to produce rays from light source

Drinking glass acts as lens and focuses light rays to a point.

theory of how lenses worked, allowing people to make lenses more accurately.

Lenses work because, when light passes from one material to another (from air to glass, then glass to air again), it is bent. By curving the lens, the **rays** of light can be made to come together at a point and produce a clear image (an image that is in **focus**, as you might say if using a camera).

The shape of the lens is vital to the image that is formed. Lenses that bulge in the centre are called **convex lenses, or converging lenses**, and they are used to magnify (*see:* **Magnification**). Lenses that are thinnest in the centre are called **concave lenses**, or diverging lenses, and make things look smaller. They have fewer uses.

Convex lenses are used in magnifying glasses, **binoculars** and cameras. The lens in the eye is also a convex lens, as are **eyeglasses**.

The type of image you get from a convex lens depends on how far from the lens you are. If you are very close to the lens, as when you wear eyeglasses, you see an upright, magnified image. If you are further away, like the film in a camera, the image is smaller and upside down. Among other things, this allows a large area to be recorded on a small piece of film.

▲ **Lens** – Many naturally bulbous transparent materials act as lenses. Raindrops are a common example.

Light

The waves of energy that can be detected by our **eyes**. The world around us gives out all kinds of energy, like heat and **sound**. But our eyes are designed to detect just a small range of waves (*see:* **Light waves** and **Sound waves**) – those whose waves are between 380 to 780 billionths of a metre long. Red

colours are made by the waves with longer lengths, then orange, yellow, green, cyan, blue and violet. Violet colours are produced by the shortest waves.

If waves throughout this range reach our eyes, we see **white light**. But if some of the waves are blocked, perhaps by a coloured glass or by the paint on a surface, we only see part of the range of waves, and that is when we see a colour. The colour we see is made of the waves that reach our eyes. So, for example, if we see 'pure' blue, we know that nearly all of the other waves have been blocked in some way. If we see a greenish blue, on the other hand, we know that a group of waves is reaching our eyes. The waves that reach our eyes and make colours are different from the waves that come directly from a light source. Waves from a light source are called **transmitted light**, and waves that bounce off a surface before they reach our eyes are called reflected light (*see:* **Reflection**).

Light travels in straight lines. You can see that when you look at **shadows**: The shadow has well-defined, not fuzzy, edges, as would be the case if light could follow a curved path. As a result, scientists can draw paths of light (called **rays**) when they are working out how light behaves when it is bounced (reflected) off a **mirror**, or when it passes through a **lens**.

(*See also:* **Absorption of light; Brightness; Diffraction of light; Dispersion of light; Doppler effect of light; Fibre optics; Interference; Light energy; Light-year; Mirage; Optics; Photon; Refraction of light; Scattering of light; Spectrum; Speed of light.**)

(*For types of light see:* **Bioluminescence; Electric light; Fluorescence; Incandescence, incandescent light; Infrared light; Luminescence; Monochromatic light; Phosphorescence; Polarised light; Skylight; Sunlight; Ultraviolet light.**)

Light bulb

(*See:* **Electric light**.)

Light energy

Light is a form of energy that can travel through empty space, or a transparent material, at very high speed. It is very different from the chemical energy stored in coal or oil, for example, which can only be transported by moving the material around. Light is, therefore, an extremely useful form of energy. It is available in huge amounts in sunshine – about 1.36 kilowatts per hour fall on every square metre at the equator, for example. The main problem is harnessing it because it has to be converted into other forms of energy, such as heat or electricity, before we can use it. So far, methods of converting light into heat and electricity have had only limited success.

To convert light into heat, huge **convex mirrors** are used to focus the light on tubes of water. The water is heated to steam, and then the steam is used to turn electricity generators. For this to be successful, a sunny site is needed.

To convert **sunlight** into electricity directly, materials called semi-conductors must be used.

Light-gathering power

The higher the **light**-gathering power of a **lens** or **mirror**, the easier it is to see small, faint objects. The light-gathering power of a **telescope** is made greater by increasing the size of the main lens or the main mirror. By doubling the diameter of a lens or mirror, the light-gathering power is increased fourfold. (*See also:* **Resolving power**.)

▶ **Lighthouse** – A tower containing a light surrounded by a number of rotating Fresnel lenses.

Lighthouse

A structure, often a tower, that acts as a beacon to warn ships of difficulties in navigation, such as shoals or the entrance to a harbour.

Most lighthouses use tungsten–halogen **lamps**, with power up to 1,500 **watts**. But a lamp on its own is not an efficient way of sending a **beam of light** up to 40km out to sea (the limit of visibility due to the curvature of the Earth). For this a system of **mirrors** and **lenses** is needed.

Concave mirrors are placed behind the **lens**. They collect **light** shining inland and convert it into a beam that is reflected out to sea.

Lenses rotate.

The lamp is placed at the **focus** of the mirror.

The light beam can be focused further by a lens placed in front of it. In 1828 Augustin-Jean Fresnel made a lens panel consisting of a central bull's-eye lens with a number of concentric glass prismatic rings (*see:* **Prism**). The panel concentrated the light into a pencil-like beam of great intensity. (*See also:* **Fresnel lens**.)

The problem with using a lens and a mirror to turn the light into a narrow beam is that it can only be seen from a small angle. To make the light visible from a wider angle, the whole lens, lamp and mirror system are rotated. As a result, the beam sweeps the horizon and is seen as a flash by people at sea. By altering the shape of the lens further, flashes of different length can be obtained. In this way the flashes can be made into a code that can identify the lighthouse.

Lighting

The way in which a room, building or other structure is illuminated. There are certain rules for lighting, but much of it is an art rather than a science. For example, lighting may have to be suitably bright for reading, but that can be provided by a number of different types of lights. The choice is a matter of what the designer wants to do.

Some of the most exciting lighting effects are outside lighting, for example, illuminating ancient buildings or the lighting used in concerts, which is often a mixture of strobe, flashing and rotating lights.

▼ **Lighting** – Light is made of waves that can be detected by the eye. They may be sources of light such as the Sun, a candle, or a light bulb (called luminous sources, or transmitted light); or the light may be reflected by other objects.

The arrangement of luminous sources and reflected surfaces determines the lighting in a room.

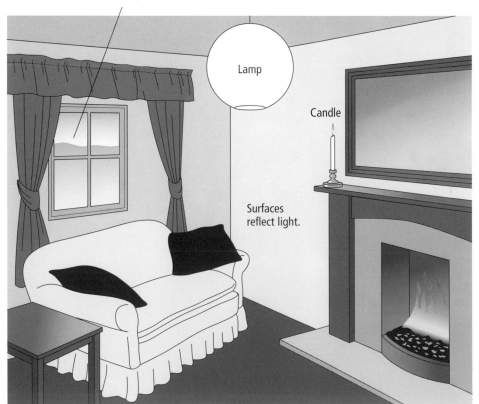

Sunlight through window

Lamp

Candle

Surfaces reflect light.

▲▶ **Lighting** – Lighting is designed for effect as well as for function. Here we see two places where the lighting is very different. The top photo shows the Manhattan, New York, skyline. Here the lighting in the buildings is mainly functional because people live or work in them. To the right is the Sydney Opera House, lit to be an attractive place to visit.

Light ray
(*See:* **Ray**.)

Light waves

Light is a form of energy. It is often thought of as a wave of energy. We can only see waves within a certain range. That is called visible light. Waves that are too short to be seen are called infrared light, and those too long to be seen are **ultraviolet light**.

Some animals see over a different range than we do and can see either infrared or ultraviolet light.

Light from a point source such as the Sun or a light bulb sends **rays**, or radiates, outwards in all directions. Because of this the amount, or intensity, of light falling on a surface lessens with the square of the distance to the source. That is why stars look dimmer than the Sun, even though the stars may be radiating thousands of times more light than our Sun. It also explains why the same light bulb seems brighter when seen close up as opposed to further away.

The light from a source such as a light bulb can be made to shine in one direction. We call it a **beam of light**. In a torch a reflector is placed behind the light and a **lens** in front of it. That produces a single beam of light. In this case the light intensity stays the same and is not affected by distance. Searchlights demonstrate this effect very well; their beam of light travels for several kilometres without widening. A laser beam can travel much farther.

(*See also:* **Photon**.)

Light-year

The distance that **light** can travel in a year. It is used to measure distances in space. Light travels at 300,000km per second. A light-year is about 9,500,000,000,000 km: nine and a half million million kilometres. Astronomers use an even larger unit called the parsec. It is about 3.262 light-years.

Loudspeaker

A device for converting electrical energy into **sound** energy within the range of **hearing** (20 to 20,000 **hertz**).

Traditionally, a loudspeaker consists of a **cone** that is made to vibrate by a special coil called a driver. This coil sits in a strong magnetic field. When an electrical signal passes through the coil, the coil makes its own magnetic field. The two magnetic fields interact, and the coil is forced to move. The moving coil is attached to the cone of the loudspeaker. The cone amplifies the movement of the coil, making it loud enough for us to hear.

Modern loudspeakers use other ways of making the cone vibrate. For example, a crystal can be made to vibrate by passing an electrical signal through it. Each method of vibration produces its own sound quality.

A single loudspeaker cannot cover the whole range of hearing,

Luminescence

Light that is produced when a special material is struck by **ultraviolet light**. That happens in a **fluorescent** tube, for example. In the tube a flow of electricity through a gas causes ultraviolet

and for this reason a number of different kinds of speakers are used, each corresponding to a particular range of vibrations. The deepest notes are reproduced by a large loudspeaker called a **woofer**. The high-**pitched** notes are reproduced by a loudspeaker called a **tweeter**. The rest of the notes are reproduced by a **midrange** loudspeaker.

(*See also:* **Amplifier**; **Distortion of sound**; **Dynamic range**.)

light to be produced. This light strikes special sensitive material on the inside of the tube, and the ultraviolet light is converted into visible light. The important thing about this process is that very little heat is given off, so the light is produced much more efficiently than through an ordinary light bulb (*see:* **Electric light**). (*See also:* **Phosphorescence**.)

Luminous

Glowing in the dark. Paint that glows in the dark is called luminous paint. It contains material that sends out **light** for a period of time after it has been illuminated.

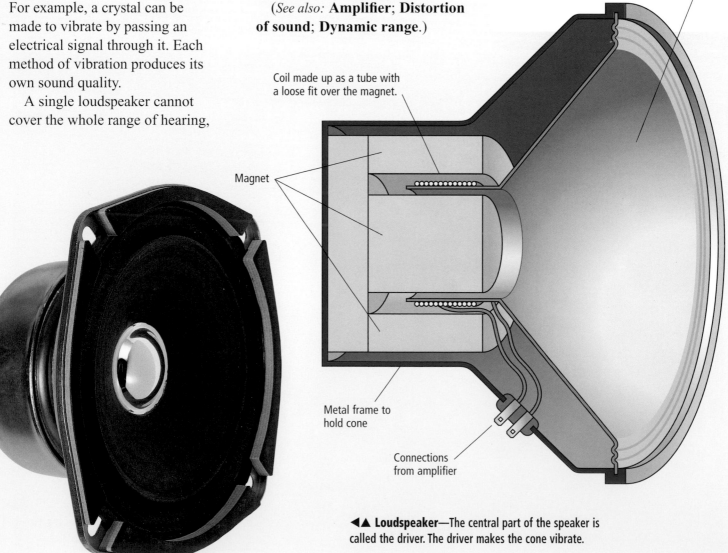

Cone made of paper or fabric

Coil made up as a tube with a loose fit over the magnet.

Magnet

Metal frame to hold cone

Connections from amplifier

◄▲ **Loudspeaker**—The central part of the speaker is called the driver. The driver makes the cone vibrate.

In the past radioactive materials were used to give a permanent glow to see-in-the-dark items like wrist-watches. These materials are now regarded as hazardous and are no longer used.

M

Magnification

Light: Making something look larger. An object can be magnified by using a **convex lens** – a **lens** that bulges out in the middle. If the lens is held close to the **eye**, an upright, magnified image can be seen.

▼ **Magnification** – A magnifying glass will often give a magnification of up to 2. For greater magnification, say to 20 or 30 times, a hand lens can be used. This is the kind of magnifier used by people such as biologists and geologists for field science. Even higher-powered magnification requires the lens to be mounted in a fixed frame because high magnification lenses have a very shallow depth of focus and so need to be focused carefully. The result is the microscope.

Magnified images are used in **microscopes** and **telescopes**. **Eyeglasses** are not usually used to provide much magnification. Their job is to make it easier to see an object clearly, and that usually just means focusing it properly.

Sound: Making something sound louder by using an **amplifying** system.

Microscope

An instrument for observing objects in detail. Microscopes use a number of **lenses** to achieve very high levels of **magnification**. They also use **mirrors** to ensure that **light** can be directed onto the subject being observed. In this way a bright, highly magnified image is achieved.

Mid-range

The size of **loudspeaker** used for reproducing the middle range of **sound**. The **cone** is normally about 6 to 10cm across. (*See also:* **Tweeter** and **Woofer**.)

◄ **Microscope** – This is a simple optical microscope.

Eyepiece

Objective lenses with a range of magnifications in a rotating block so that the user can switch from one to another

The thing being viewed is held on a specimen table in the focal plane for the lenses.

A lens is used to concentrate the reflected light source onto the thing being viewed.

A mirror is used to reflect the light source up into the specimen.

Mirage

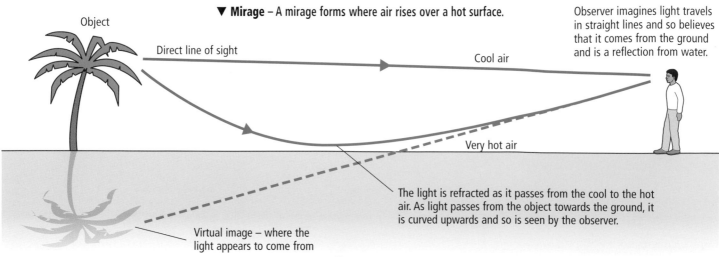

Object

Direct line of sight

Cool air

Very hot air

Observer imagines light travels in straight lines and so believes that it comes from the ground and is a reflection from water.

The light is refracted as it passes from the cool to the hot air. As light passes from the object towards the ground, it is curved upwards and so is seen by the observer.

Virtual image – where the light appears to come from

Mirage

An optical illusion produced by hot air rising from the ground. On a hot day the air close to the ground is warmed more than the air above. As **light** passes through this warm air, it is bent back upwards because the properties of warm air are different from cold air (just as the properties of glass are different from air). The bending of light makes us see both a distant object directly and also the image of the object made by the bending of **rays** in the hot air layer close to the ground. That produces a **mirror** effect in which both an object and its **reflection** are visible. We are used to seeing reflections in water, so we imagine that the reflection is produced by a lake or puddle. That is the mirage.

Mirror

A surface that reflects **light** well and that can be used to see objects. Many mirrors are flat. They consist of a sheet of glass with silver or aluminium coating on the back. The glass protects the metal from becoming dull due to contact with the air. The glass itself plays no part in the mirror effect.

Mirrors can be made that bulge outwards (**convex mirrors**), or that

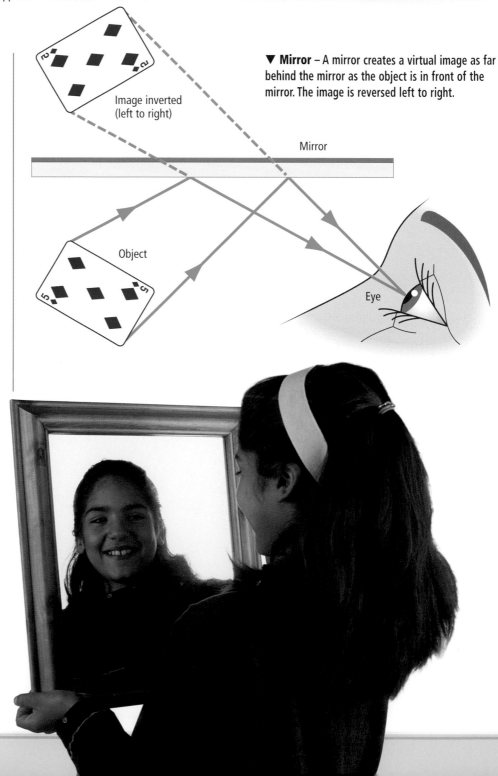

Image inverted (left to right)

Mirror – A mirror creates a virtual image as far behind the mirror as the object is in front of the mirror. The image is reversed left to right.

Mirror

Object

Eye

dip inwards (**concave mirrors**). Convex mirrors are used for security in shops because they provide a wide field of view. Concave mirrors are used to reflect light from a bulb in a torch and help produce a **beam**. Curved mirrors with a slightly more complicated shape (called parabolic mirrors) are used to gather light from distant stars and **focus** it at a point. That makes the star easier to see. (*See also:* **Angle of incidence** and **Angle of reflection**.)

Monochromatic light

The **light** of a single **colour**, not white, which is a mixture of all colours, or black, which is the absence of light.

Munsell system

A system for identifying **colours** by certain properties. It is extremely useful if colours need to be matched, such as in printing, dyeing and painting.

Musical instrument

Anything that is designed to play a sequence of pleasing **sounds**. All musical instruments rely on the vibration of air within our range of **hearing**. That can be achieved in many ways.

In 500 B.C. Pythagoras noticed that the shorter the plucked string of a lyre, the higher the **pitch** of the sound it produced. He also discovered that pleasing sounds were produced when strings of different length were plucked. One particularly pleasant ratio was found when one string was exactly twice the length of the other. We now know that this difference is an **octave**, the basis of our musical scales. Holding the string down

halfway down its length produces the same result as having a short string. That is how the fingerboard on a stringed instrument works.

Strings with lengths in the ratio of 2 to 3 or 3 to 4 also worked well. These ratios are now known as a fifth and a fourth.

Musical notes can be played not only by string instruments such as the violin, the cello, the double bass, the guitar and the harp, but also by instruments that use vibrating **reeds**, such as the accordion, or by a combination of vibrating reeds and resonating air columns such as the clarinet, the bassoon and the saxophone. The lips can be shaped like a reed, allowing **brass** instruments such as the bugle, the trumpet, the trombone and the tuba to be played.

Blowing over a hole in a pipe will also produce sounds in instruments such as the organ, the flute and the recorder.

Drums use vibrating skins to produce sound. Hammers strike the metal of bells, chimes and glockenspiels.

(*See also:* **Percussion**; **Tuning fork**; **Wind instrument**; **Woodwind**.)

▼ **Musical instrument** – A musical instrument, such as a violin, is designed to produce pleasing notes consisting of fundamentals and harmonics. The fingers are used to change the length of the vibrating string, and thus the frequency, and so produce a variety of notes. The vibration occurs over a sounding box that serves to reverberate and amplify the sound. The design of the case affects the nature of the harmonics and the 'colour,' or quality, of the sound.

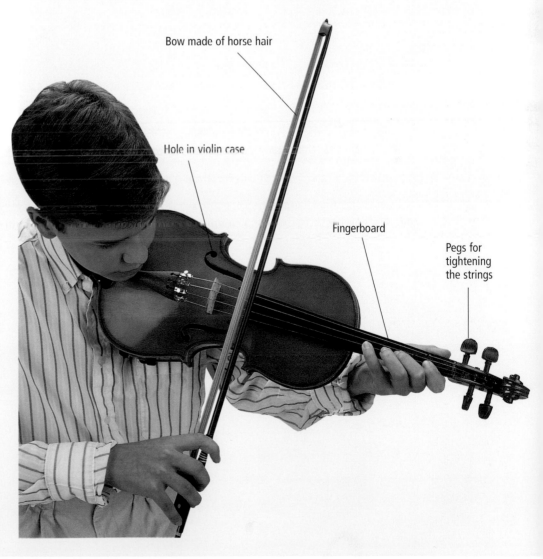

Bow made of horse hair

Hole in violin case

Fingerboard

Pegs for tightening the strings

N

Newton's rings
(*See:* **Interference**.)

Noise
Any unwanted **sound**. It may be a loud sound that disturbs the listener. In radios noise is unwanted electrical signals that accompany the desired signal. They are sometimes called 'static' because such noise is often generated by lightning and other sources of sparks. The equivalent on a television picture is called 'snow'. (*See also:* **Pink noise** and **White noise**.)

O

Octave
A musical interval that forms the unit of the modern scale. An octave is a fundamental unit used in nearly all music no matter what culture it comes from. In western music an octave contains eight notes.

The note at the top of an octave has twice the **frequency** of the note at the bottom. A one-octave step stretches, for example, from the note C (261 **hertz**) to its octave C' (522 hertz). The octave from the note A stretches from A (220 hertz) to its octave A' (440 hertz).

A child has a **hearing** range of more than 10 octaves. A piano keyboard has an octave range of 7.5 octaves.

It is also possible to talk about **light** in terms of octaves. The range of human sight is much more limited than the range of hearing. It spans just one octave, the lowest frequency light being just half of the highest frequency light that we can see. We call it the **spectrum**.

Optics
The science of studying **light**.

Overtone
A **musical instrument** will produce a **fundamental tone**, for example, middle C. When this note is played, a range of overtones will also be produced that are at **frequencies** higher than the fundamental tone. They combine with the fundamental tone to give the **sound** richness.

In most instruments, for example, **woodwinds** and strings, the overtones are exact multiples, or **harmonics**, of the fundamental tone. On a piano the overtones are not all exact multiples of the fundamental. these features are responsible for the special characteristic of piano sound. (*See also:* **Timbre** and **Wavelength**.)

▼ **Overtone** – A complete wavelength is a fundamental. One-half a wavelength is a first overtone, one-third of a wavelength is a second overtone, and so on.

P

Percussion
A range of **musical instruments** in which a skin (in the case of instruments like drums) or a metal (as in a xylophone or handbells) are struck sharply to cause a vibration.

Period
The time it takes for a complete wave to pass. It is the inverse of the **frequency** (period = 1/frequency).

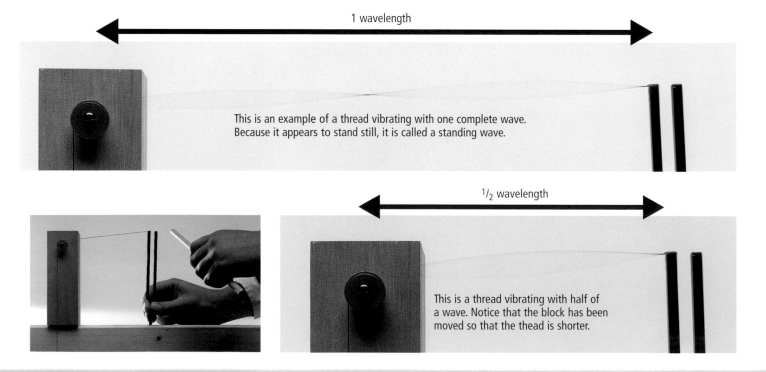

1 wavelength

This is an example of a thread vibrating with one complete wave. Because it appears to stand still, it is called a standing wave.

$1/2$ wavelength

This is a thread vibrating with half of a wave. Notice that the block has been moved so that the thead is shorter.

Tom-toms: the main drums. They are relatively small drums and so vibrate when they are struck to produce a high note. The skin is pulled tight so that it comes to rest quickly after being struck. This makes short notes that can be played rapidly.

Cymbal: This single cymbal is struck with the drumstick.

▶▼ Percussion instruments – Drums are an obvious form of percussion, but pianos also use percussion – they work by striking a string sharply with a hammer.

Hi-hat: A pair of cymbals that are moved up and down on a rod. The hi-hat is worked from a lever on the floor.

Floor tom

Snare drum: A drum with a set of wires placed on the drum skin. It makes a more rattling sound when played.

Bass drum: This drum makes a deeper, more booming, and longer-lasting sound. That is because it vibrates more slowly than the other, smaller drums.

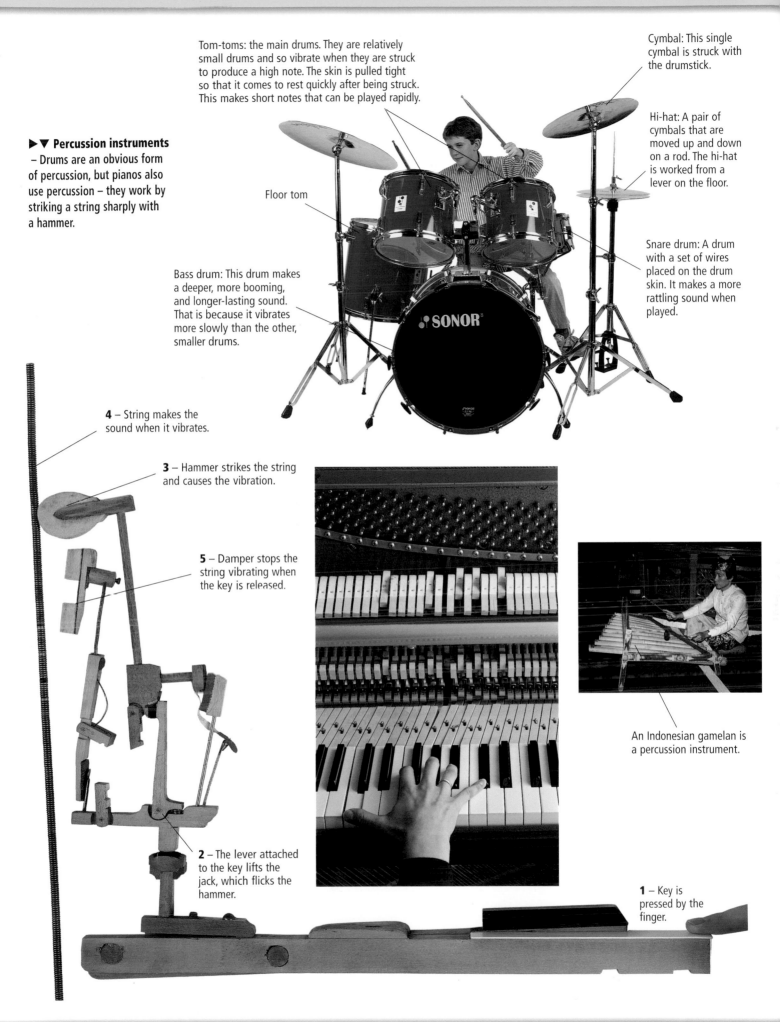

4 – String makes the sound when it vibrates.

3 – Hammer strikes the string and causes the vibration.

5 – Damper stops the string vibrating when the key is released.

2 – The lever attached to the key lifts the jack, which flicks the hammer.

An Indonesian gamelan is a percussion instrument.

1 – Key is pressed by the finger.

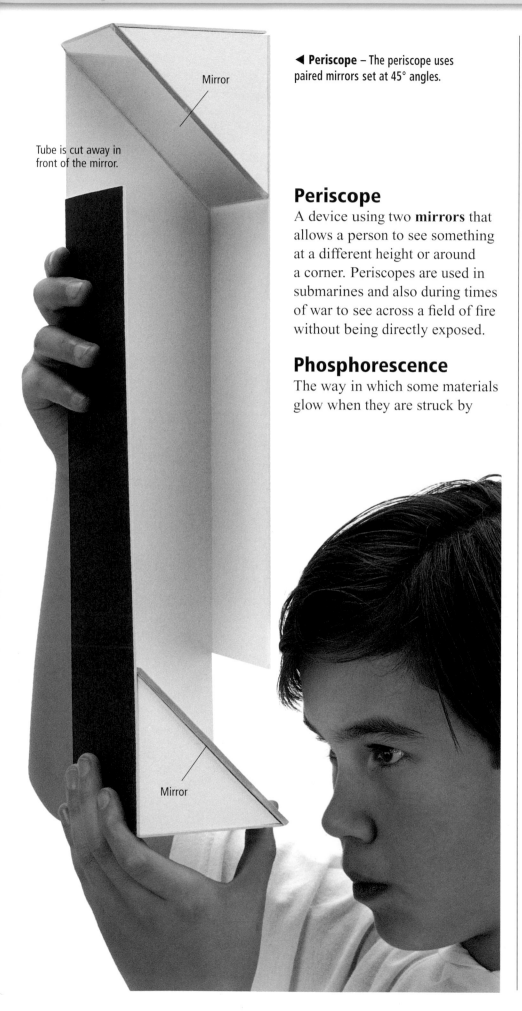

Mirror

Tube is cut away in front of the mirror.

◀ **Periscope** – The periscope uses paired mirrors set at 45° angles.

Mirror

Periscope

A device using two **mirrors** that allows a person to see something at a different height or around a corner. Periscopes are used in submarines and also during times of war to see across a field of fire without being directly exposed.

Phosphorescence

The way in which some materials glow when they are struck by invisible waves such as **ultraviolet light**. (*See also:* **Fluorescence** and **Luminescence**.)

Photoelectric effect

The ability of some materials to change **light** into electricity. Substances like selenium are especially useful in this respect, and they are used in photocells. Currently photocells are not efficient enough to produce more than the small amounts of power needed to run such things as calculators or space vehicles. It is hoped that, eventually, banks of photocells will be able to produce enough power to replace fossil fuels like oil and coal.

Photon

The basic source of **light**. It is a very tiny package of **light energy**. When a hot object releases a photon, we see it as a wave of light.

Pigment

A substance in the form of tiny particles suspended in a liquid that scatters certain kinds of **light** better than others (*see:* **Scattering of light**). Paint consists of a liquid (called a body) into which the pigment is mixed to produce the desired **colour**.

The size of the pigment particles is important. Tiny particles produce a glossy finish to paint, while larger particles give a matt finish.

Pink noise

Random **noise** in the range of 20 to 20,000Hz. The result is a hissing **sound** that drowns out all other kinds of sound. (*See also:* **White noise**.)

Pitch

Another word for **frequency**. (*See also:* **Doppler effect of sound**.)

Polarised light

Light whose waves move in just one plane. **Light waves** normally arrive from many angles and are not polarised. Light becomes polarised when it passes through or bounces off certain substances. Water and metal turn ordinary light into polarised light. Polarising sunglasses make use of this effect to eliminate the polarised light bounced from metal and water. That takes away the glare that polarisation produces.

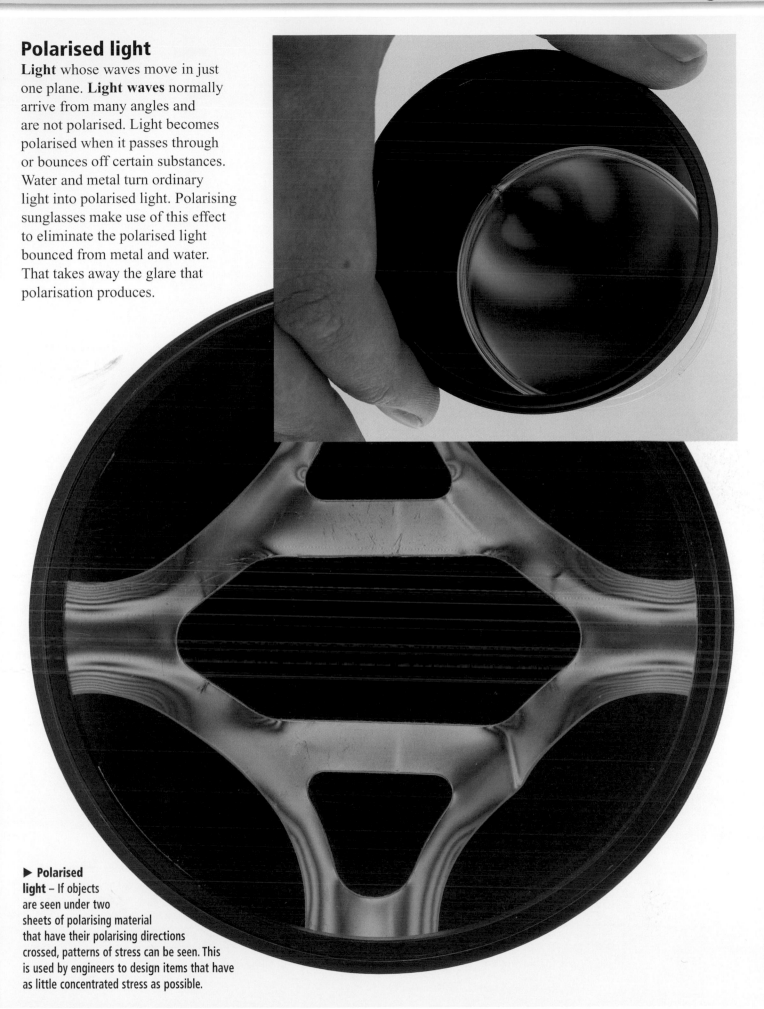

▶ **Polarised light** – If objects are seen under two sheets of polarising material that have their polarising directions crossed, patterns of stress can be seen. This is used by engineers to design items that have as little concentrated stress as possible.

Primary colours

The three **colours** from which all other colours can be made. They are red, green and blue. That is why, for example, the glowing dots on the inside of a television screen are designed to give out red, green and blue light.

When **light** is sent directly to the **eye**, the primary colours appear to add together. Red and green make yellow. Green and blue produce cyan. Blue and red make magenta. Red, green and blue produce white.

However, when light reflected from the world around us reaches the eye, the primary colours are different. The primaries become magenta (bluish-red), yellow and cyan (blue–green).

These reflected primary colours absorb some of the **white light** that reaches them and filter out, or subtract, certain **light waves**. These primaries are the opposite (called **complementary**) colours from the red, green and blue primaries. For example, a magenta filter will take out the green part of the light, while a yellow filter takes out the blue and cyan takes out the red. If you placed a magenta filter over a yellow filter and then added a cyan filter, or if you added magenta to yellow or cyan **dyes**, no light would leave at all. That is how the black colour of paint is created. (*See also:* **Colour mixing**.)

Prism

A wedge-shaped piece of glass or plastic. Prisms have played an important part in the study of **light**. They were used by Sir Isaac Newton to separate **white light** into a **rainbow** of **colours** (*see:* **Primary colours**). Using a prism, he was able to show that white light was not a single colour at all, but a mixture of all other colours.

Prisms are still used in science to make rainbows, or **spectrums**, of coloured light **beams**.

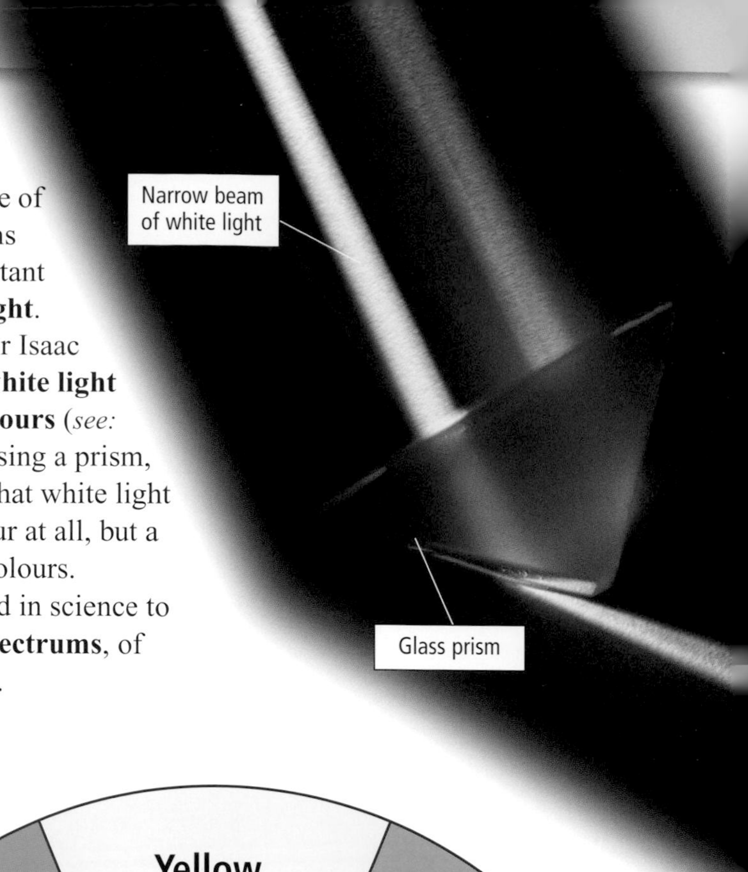

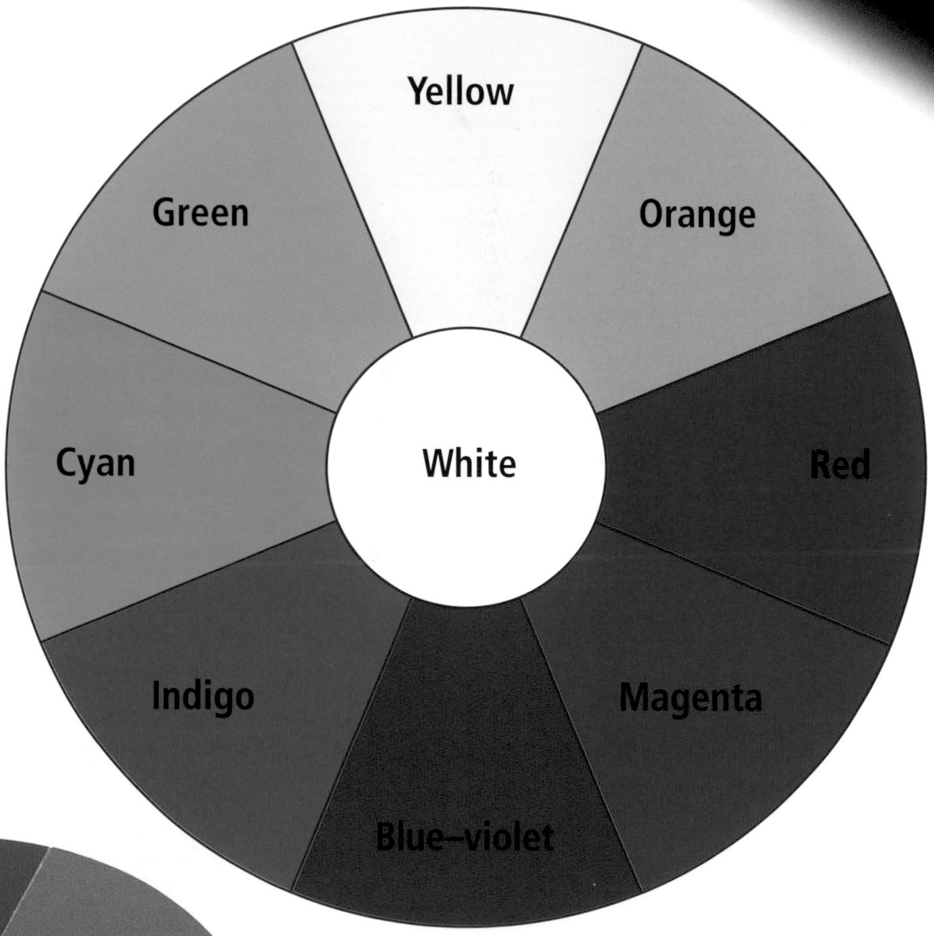

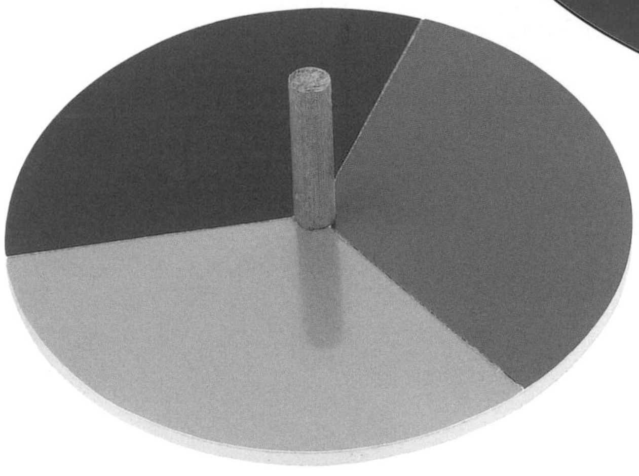

◀▲ **Primary colours** – The primary colours are red, green, and blue. If they are placed on a spinning top, as shown left, the colours will appear to merge together to make white.

The primary colours all have complementary colours. They are shown in a diagram first devised by Sir Isaac Newton.

Prisms are also used to reflect light. Pairs of prisms are used inside **binoculars** to shorten the tubes of the binoculars. Without the prisms to bend the light back on itself, binoculars would have to be as long as **telescopes**.

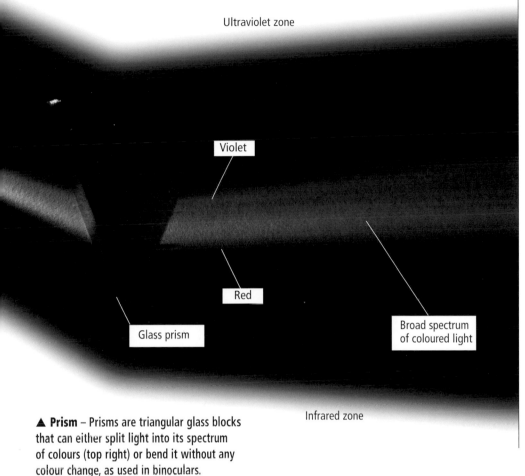

Ultraviolet zone

Violet

Red

Glass prism

Broad spectrum of coloured light

Infrared zone

▲ **Prism** – Prisms are triangular glass blocks that can either split light into its spectrum of colours (top right) or bend it without any colour change, as used in binoculars.

▼ **Rainbow** – A rainbow is produced by reflection and refraction inside raindrops.

Rainbow

Curved bands of coloured **light** produced when the sun shines on raindrops falling from a cloud or passes through water droplets in mist and fog. Rainbows are produced by the way that the **sunlight** is bent as it passes through the drops. As light enters a drop of water, the water bends, or refracts, each **colour** in the **white light** differently. When the light comes out of the drop, it is no longer white light, but split up into its colours.

The sharpest rainbow is called a primary rainbow. The colours in a rainbow are (from inside to outside) violet, indigo, blue, green, yellow orange and red.

A weaker rainbow is formed by **rays** that have been bounced around the inside of a raindrop twice. They emerge at a slightly different angle and so are seen beyond the primary rainbow. In this rainbow the colours are reversed. Even weaker rainbows can also often be seen.

You can only see a rainbow when you have your back to the Sun.

Ray, ray diagram

The path that a thin **beam of light** would take. A ray diagram is used by scientists to plot the path that single beams of **light** would take. That helps in finding out how **lenses** and **mirrors** behave. Most of the diagrams in this book are ray diagrams.

A ray diagram for a convex lens

Object O

F

F

Image, I

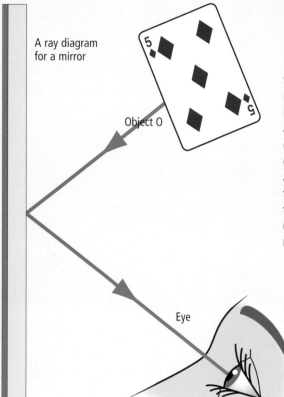

A ray diagram for a mirror

Object O

Eye

◀▲ **Ray, ray diagram** – These two diagrams illustrate how two rays are drawn to find the way light behaves. When working with a mirror, a single ray may be enough. When working with a lens, one ray is drawn from the top of an object parallel to the axis of the lens and the second through the centre of the mirror. The focus (image) of the object is where the rays meet.

▲▼ **Reed** – These are reeds from musical instruments. The bagpipes are a reed instrument.

Real image

An image that can be seen on a sheet of paper or made into a photograph. A real image is produced by a **convex lens**, which bulges in the centre, providing the source of **light** is at some distance from the **lens**. A real image is upside down and back to front. You can see that by opening the back of a **camera** and looking through the lens while the shutter is open (take out any film first).

Reed

A thin blade of cane or metal placed between a **musical instrument** player's mouth and the sound chamber of the instrument. When the player blows across the reed, it makes the reed vibrate, setting up a vibration in the air of the sound chamber.

The simplest reed is called a ribbon reed. It is a blade of grass that is held taut in front of the player's mouth. When air is blown over the reed, it vibrates and produces a harsh squawking **sound**.

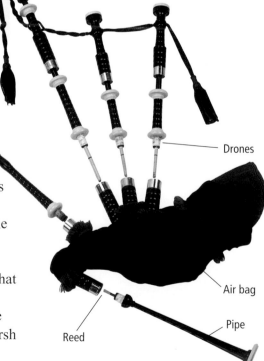

Drones

Air bag

Pipe

Reed

Reed instruments, such as clarinets and oboes, have reeds set in pipes. The pipe length controls the **pitch** of the instrument and improves the **tone** of the notes. Different notes are produced by changing the length of the pipe by opening or closing valves or finger holes.

Reflection

When a **beam of light** strikes a surface, it may go through the surface, or it may be bounced off.

If the **light** is bounced, it is said to be reflected.

If the light is coloured, the effect of reflection will be to change the **colour** of the light because some colours will usually be absorbed more than others. Gold, for example, appears orange-yellow simply because it reflects more orange–yellow light than any other kind of light. Copper appears orange–brown because it reflects more of these colours than any other colour.

Most metals reflect a large part of the light that falls on them, which is why they appear shiny (called metallic lustre). **Mirrors** are made of either silver or aluminium coated onto glass. The glass is only there to protect the metal.

In transparent materials the direction in which light strikes the surface is also very important in determining whether or not light will be reflected. We all know that we can see through glass if we look through it more or less

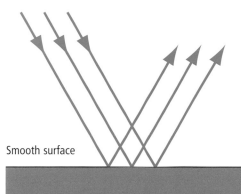

Smooth surface

◄► **Reflection** – When light bounces off a surface, it is reflected. If the surface is completely smooth, the light rays rebound in parallel, and the result is a mirror. Most surfaces are not as smooth as a mirror, and light bounces from them irregularly. That is why they have a more matte appearance. Nevertheless, they all reflect light.

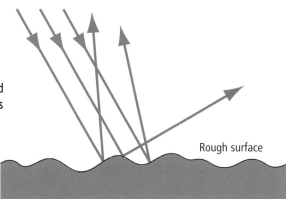

Rough surface

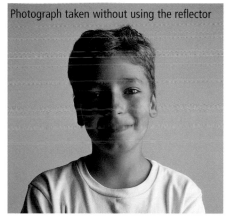

Photograph taken without using the reflector

Photograph taken using the reflector

◄▼ **Reflection** – Because light travels in straight lines, illuminating a subject for a portrait shot using just one light source will leave one part of the subject in shadow. That can be compensated for by using a very reflective surface to bounce some light back to the side in shadow. The same principle can be used to brighten dark walls in a room.

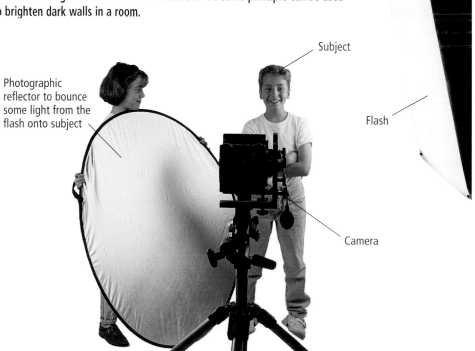

Subject

Photographic reflector to bounce some light from the flash onto subject

Flash

Camera

directly. But if we look through glass at an angle, we can no longer see through it, and it behaves as though it were a mirror. The largest angle at which the glass still appears transparent is called the **critical angle**.

For a surface to behave like a mirror, it must be very smooth. If it is rough, like the surface of a wooden table, the light will be scattered in many directions, and we will not be able to see a reflection (*see:* **Scattering of light**). By polishing a table, some of the depressions in the wood are filled with polish, and the surface becomes smoother. As a result, it becomes more mirror-like. Wax does the same job on car paint.

If an object does not absorb one kind of **light wave** in preference to others, all of the light is reflected, and it appears white in white light, blue in blue light and so on. If very little light is absorbed, the object will appear transparent, as is the case for glass. If an object absorbs all light uniformly, it will appear black. Depending on how much light is absorbed, the object will appear as darker or lighter shades of grey.

For something to look truly red, less than 10% of the red light must be absorbed, but over 90% of all other kinds of light. If the red light is absorbed only slightly less than the other waves, the object will still look a greyish-red. Greyish-blues and greens result in the same way. (*See also:* **Absorption of light**.)

Sound can be reflected in the same way as light. In this case the surface does not have to be shiny or obviously reflective, just smooth and hard.

Just as light can be brought to a **focus** by a curved mirror, sound can be brought to a focus

by a room with curved walls. All whispering galleries have curved walls, allowing a person to whisper in one part of the gallery and be heard on the opposite side.

Ray of light

Glass block

Ray of light

Refraction of light

When **light** passes from one transparent substance to another, it is often bent. That is called refraction. Refraction can be seen by placing a straw in a glass of water. The straw appears to bend

◀▼ **Refraction of light** – Refraction makes the straw appear to be bent as it enters the water. Refraction through glass makes the light be bent twice. It emerges from the block in the same direction as it enters, but displaced to one side.

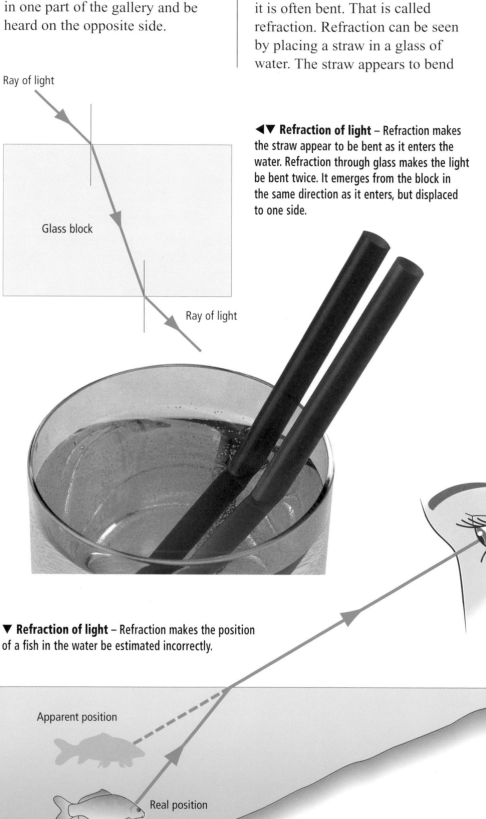

▼ **Refraction of light** – Refraction makes the position of a fish in the water be estimated incorrectly.

Apparent position

Real position

Due to refraction, the fish appears to be at a shallower depth that it actually is.

where it goes into the water. Once light has passed from one substance to another, it continues in a straight line. The bending only happens at the surface. If light passes from air into a glass block, it will be bent as it enters the glass and again when it leaves. As it leaves the glass, it is bent by the same amount as when it entered, so it leaves in the same direction as it enters, although not in quite the same path. The same thing happens when light passes from air to water in clouds.

The amount by which the light is bent depends on the length of the **light waves**. Red waves are bent by a different amount than blue waves. If the light passes through a straight-sided sheet of glass, this difference is removed because the light is bent back when it leaves the glass. However, when light passes through a raindrop or a glass without parallel sides (a **prism**), it gives rise to a **rainbow**. (*See also:* **Angle of refraction**.) (*Compare with:* **Diffraction of light**.)

Refraction of sound

The bending of **sound waves** as they travel through different kinds of medium. **Sound** travels faster through warm air than through cool air. During the day the ground is hotter than the air above. That makes the wave travel in a curve upwards, quickly taking the sound out of **hearing**. At night the situation is reversed and the sound is deflected downwards, allowing people to hear more clearly and for greater distances than by day. (*See also:* **Diffraction of sound**.)

Resolving power

The ability to tell closely spaced objects apart. It is related to the size of the main, or objective, **lens** in a **telescope**. The bigger the objective lens, the better the resolving power.

Resonance

A reinforcement of vibration that occurs when two objects vibrate in step. Resonance of air can occur in the tube of a **wind instrument** or can be transmitted between objects when they are touching.

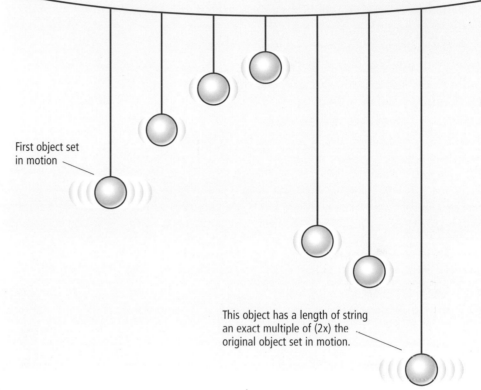

▼ **Resonance** – Every object has a natural frequency of vibration, and it can be started up by another object vibrating nearby. In this diagram the object that vibrates most strongly is that which has a length of string that is a multiple of the length of string of the object that was originally set in motion.

First object set in motion

This object has a length of string an exact multiple of (2x) the original object set in motion.

Retina

The inner surface of the back of the **eye**. It is covered in **light**-sensitive cells in the shape of **cones** and rods.

Reverberation

The **sounds** reflected from walls and ceilings that reach the listener fractionally after the direct sound. If the time delay between the direct sound and the reflected sounds is more than 0.05 seconds, the sounds can be heard distinctly and are called **echoes**.

Reverberation is strong in places like churches and much organ music relies on reverberation from the walls for its effect.

Reverberation accounts for the time a sound takes to **decay** (fade away). It is part of the **acoustics** of a room.

S

Saturation

The property of a **colour** that determines how vivid it looks. It compares the colour to a grey at the same level of **brightness**.

Scattering of light

When **light** passes through a substance, some of it is soaked up (*see:* **Absorption of light**), but much more is bounced off in all directions (*see:* **Reflection**). Imagine light passing through a cloud containing billions of tiny water droplets. Light hits a droplet and a tiny amount of light goes straight through. Most bounces off the surface of the drop and heads off in a new direction. Smoke does the same thing, as do all gases, including air. Tiny imperfections in a crystal will also scatter light.

The amount of scattering depends on the **wavelength** (**colour**) of the light. It is the reason the sky appears blue. **Sunlight** is scattered as it passes through the air. The blue light is scattered much more than the red light, so that sunlight has less blue than if we saw it from space. That is why sunlight appears slightly yellow. The blue light continues to be bounced around in the air and eventually reaches the **eye**. Because it is mostly blue light that is scattered, the sky appears blue.

Skylight

The bluish-coloured **light** that we see in a clear sky. It is produced by air molecules **scattering** the sunlight so that more blue light is scattered in the sky than any other **colour**. From Earth the Sun looks yellower than it does from space because some of the blue in sunlight has been scattered away into the air.

Space appears black because there are too few particles to scatter the sunlight.

Sonar

(*See:* **Ultrasound**.)

Sonic boom

When an aeroplane is moving relatively slowly, there is plenty of time for the air molecules to get out of the way. However, as the aeroplane reaches the **speed of sound**, it overtakes the moving molecules and compresses the layers of air in its line of flight. At the speed of sound the waves become audible as a sonic boom.

The ratio of the speed of an object to the speed of sound is called the Mach number, after the Austrian physicist Ernst Mach. Mach 1 is the speed of sound.

Shadow

The absence of **light** caused by an object blocking the path of light **rays**. Because light travels in straight lines, the edges of a shadow are sharp. The size of the shadow depends on the distance between the object blocking light and the source of light, and on the distance between the object and the surface on which the light falls. The closer the object is to the light, and the further away the surface is, the bigger the shadow.

The Sun produces shadows that vary in direction and length during the day and also between seasons. When the Sun is low in the sky, the top of the shadow is a long way from the observer, and the shadow appears stretched. When the Sun is nearly overhead, the shadow appears squashed.

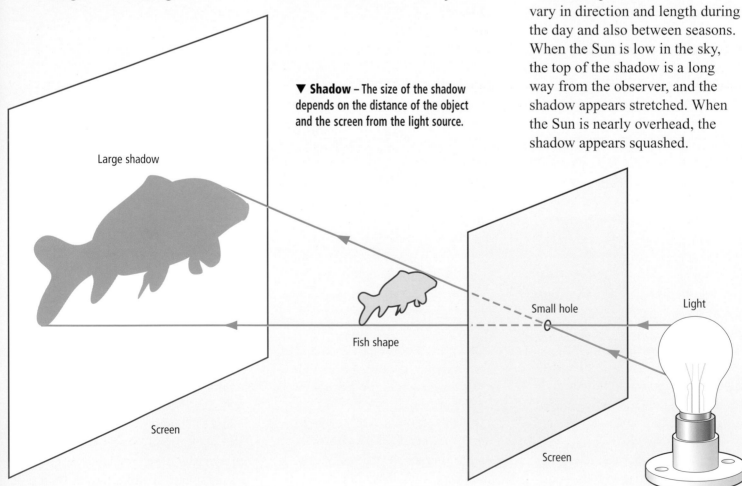

▼ **Shadow** – The size of the shadow depends on the distance of the object and the screen from the light source.

Large shadow

Fish shape

Screen

Small hole

Light

Screen

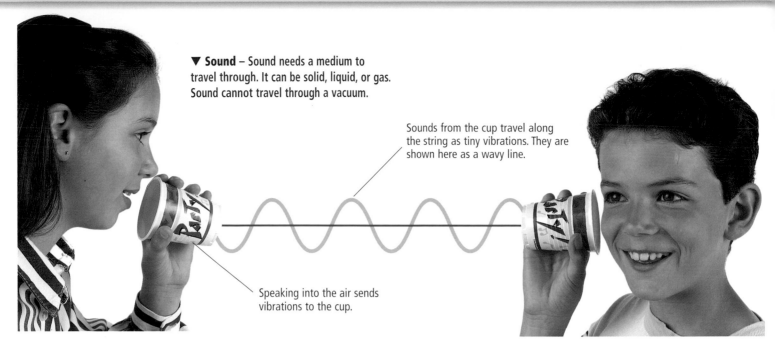

▼ **Sound** – Sound needs a medium to travel through. It can be solid, liquid, or gas. Sound cannot travel through a vacuum.

Sounds from the cup travel along the string as tiny vibrations. They are shown here as a wavy line.

Speaking into the air sends vibrations to the cup.

Sound

Any vibration through a material, either a gas, a liquid, or a solid.

Sound, unlike **light**, must have a medium to travel through. That can be demonstrated by placing a bell in a flask and then pumping out the air. As the number of air molecules is reduced, the sound weakens until, when there is a vacuum in the flask, the bell cannot be heard ringing at all.

We cannot detect the same range of sounds as other living things. For example, dogs can hear a dog whistle that is too high a **frequency** for human **ears**. Sonar (**ultrasound**), used to detect objects underwater, is also a **sound wave** out of the range of human **hearing**.

When a sound reaches our ears, it puts slight pressure on the diaphragm of the ear, and that in turn causes changes in the ear that send electrical signals to the brain.

Sound waves move through different materials at different speeds. Sound moves at different speeds through gases, liquids and solids. The **speed of sound** in dry air at 0°C is about 33m/s. The speed of sound in seawater is 1,490m/s. In steel the speed of sound is 5,000m/s.

Sound is measured by its **wavelength**, its frequency and its intensity. The peak value of each wave is measured in **watts** per square centimetre.

(*See also:* **Acoustics**; **Decibel**; **Distortion of sound**; **Diffraction of sound**; **Doppler effect of sound**; **Echo**; **Hertz (Hz)**; **Loudspeaker**; **Musical instrument**; **Noise**; **Refraction of sound**; **Reverberation**; **Sound level**; **Soundproofing**; **Spectrum**; **Timbre**; **Tone**.)

Sound level

You hear **sound** because a wave of air pressure makes your eardrum move. This power can be measured in **watts**. Sound levels can also be described in terms of **decibels** (dB). On the decibel scale the smallest sound that can be heard is 0dB. This sound has an intensity of about 15 watts per square centimetre. Sound becomes painful (because the pressure on the **ear** is too great) at about 135dB.

The decibel scale does not rise evenly; instead, the pressure doubles for each 3dB increase. The difference between a 5W **amplifier** and a 10W amplifier is

3dB. Between the quietest sound that can be heard and pain, the pressure doubles about 45 times. The highest level the ear can tolerate is 1,000 billion times the quietest. That is an amazing range of sound levels – called a **dynamic range** and far beyond anything a **loudspeaker** is capable of generating. In a totally quiet environment the ear is so sensitive that it can just pick up the sound of blood flowing in the ear. At this level the eardrum vibrates a distance smaller than the diameter of a hydrogen molecule.

Music levels vary from about 50dB for quiet background music to 100dB for a full orchestra all playing together, to 120dB for a very loud rock band.

The human ear is most sensitive to sounds in the range of 20Hz to 20,000Hz (20kHz), the normal range of speech.

An orchestra covers sound levels from 20dB in quiet passages to 100dB in the loudest parts. If you were to record this on disc or tape, you would need a system that covers a range of 80dB. The old long-playing records (vinyl) reach 50 to 70dB; a CD can cover 96dB.

Soundproofing

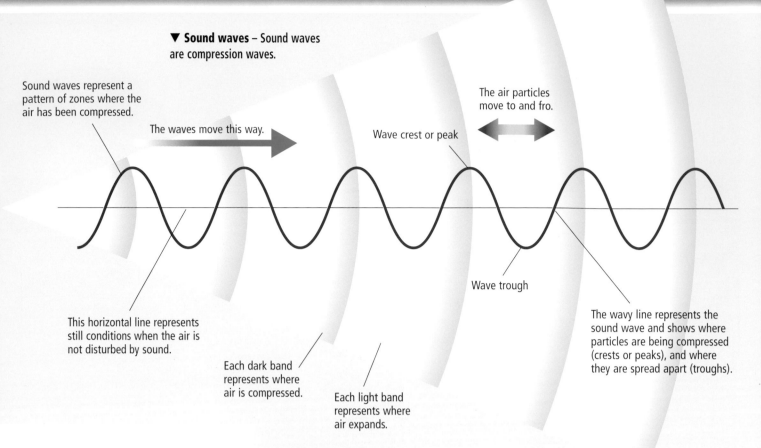

▼ Sound waves – Sound waves are compression waves.

Sound waves represent a pattern of zones where the air has been compressed.

The waves move this way.

Wave crest or peak

The air particles move to and fro.

Wave trough

This horizontal line represents still conditions when the air is not disturbed by sound.

Each dark band represents where air is compressed.

Each light band represents where air expands.

The wavy line represents the sound wave and shows where particles are being compressed (crests or peaks), and where they are spread apart (troughs).

Soundproofing

Reducing the **sound** that is transmitted through walls and windows so that the source of sound is contained in a room as well as possible.

When **sound waves** travel through the air and strike a room wall, floor, or ceiling, the partition then acts like a diaphragm and transmits the sounds to adjoining rooms.

Soundproofing efficiency depends on the density of the wall material. A wall made from masonry will act as a better soundproof barrier than one made of wallboards on a wooden frame. To increase soundproofing in hollow walls, a sound-absorbing filler can be added.

Materials with small holes (porous materials) absorb sound energy much more effectively than flat materials. Fibre tiles and panels, special acoustical plasters and polyurethane foam are all effective soundproofing materials. (*See also:* **Damping**.)

Sound waves

A travelling pattern, or wave, consisting of regions of high and low pressure through air or some other medium that can be detected by our **ears**. The changes in pressure are caused by places where molecules become compacted and regions where they are relatively scarce.

Every space contains a vast number of air molecules. The living room of a house might contain over one billion billion billion (10 followed by 20 zeros, or 10^{20}) air molecules. If you could weigh them, you would find they weighed about 70 to 80kg. Nevertheless, there is much more empty space between the air molecules than is taken up by the molecules themselves, and so the molecules are still free to move around.

Air molecules look like small spinning dumbbells and are moving around at about 1,600km/h, colliding with one another all

of the time. In still air the molecules move around randomly, each molecule colliding with its neighbours about 5 billion times a second. The amount of energy of movement of these molecules is amazing, being greater than the energy used by four large cars travelling at top speed. And all this in a still room!

The pressure of air molecules on a human eardrum is about 300kg per square metre (the same as four large people). However, this great pressure does not destroy the eardrum because there is an equal pressure from molecules inside the **ear**.

If a **sound** is played in the room, the air molecules no longer move randomly. A note like an A, which is about 400 cycles per second, sets up 400 waves per second travelling across the room, each about a metre apart, at a speed of 12,000km/h – the **speed of sound**.

You don't get bombarded by

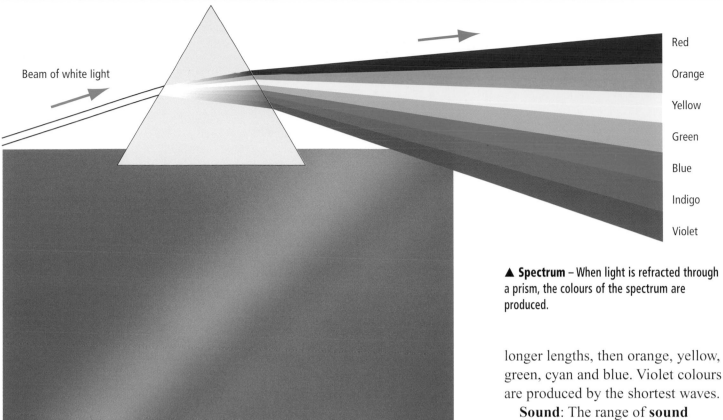

Beam of white light

Red
Orange
Yellow
Green
Blue
Indigo
Violet

▲ **Spectrum** – When light is refracted through a prism, the colours of the spectrum are produced.

▲ **Spectrum** – The spectrum can be seen in a rainbow.

Speaker
(*See.* **Loudspeaker**.)

Spectacles
(*See:* **Eyeglasses**.)

Spectrum
A range of **frequencies**.

Light: The range of **light waves** that our eyes can see – separated out. This happens in the sky to produce a **rainbow** and also in a glass block called a **prism**. Red **colours** are made by the waves with longer lengths, then orange, yellow, green, cyan and blue. Violet colours are produced by the shortest waves.

Sound: The range of **sound waves** that we can hear, normally from 20Hz to 20kHz.

Speed of light
Light does not travel instantly from one place to another. It takes time for the **light waves** to get from their source to their destination. However, light travels so fast (about 300,000 kilometres per second) that we do not notice this delay when we turn on a light. It is only noticeable over long distances.

Astronomers know that it takes light a long time to reach us from other parts of the universe. They use this knowledge to measure distances in **light-years**. The furthest objects we can detect are billions of light-years away from us. The light we see from them now was generated billions of years ago. In this way we are seeing what the universe was like billions of years ago. We have no idea what it is like today because light produced from these vast distances away will not reach us until billions of years in the future. (*See also:* **Index of refraction**.)

molecules and splattered against the wall, however, because the molecules pass on their energy in a domino effect. It's the same as using a 'slinky coil'. The energy goes in one end, moves all of the coils back and forth, and comes out at the other end. In air the sound source compresses the molecules next to it, which then compress the ones next to them and so on until it reaches the listener.

A wave doesn't compress the molecules very much as it travels, but it does cause a change in the pressure on the ear. The loudest sound you can tolerate adds about 0.05kg per sq m of pressure. But since the pressure on your inner ear is balanced for still air, the extra pressure of the wave causes the eardrum to be pushed very slightly each time the wave arrives. Once the wave has passed, the eardrum springs back and is then pushed in by the next wave. In this way the waves make the eardrum vibrate and pass a message to the inner ear.

Sound waves behave like **light waves** in many ways. Sound waves can, for example, be reflected, or bounced, from objects, just like light waves. (*See also:* **Decay** and **Frequency**.)

Speed of sound

The speed at which **sound** moves is slow compared with that of **light**. That is why there is a time interval between seeing a flash of lightning and **hearing** the crack of thunder.

Sound can only be heard through a gas (such as air), a liquid (such as water), or a solid (such as steel). Sound does not travel through a vacuum and so does not travel through space.

In 1738 French scientists set up a cannon on one hill and observed it from 27 kilometres away. They timed how long it took to hear the explosion after seeing the flash of gunpowder. The distance divided by the time gave them the speed of sound.

The speed of sound in air at 0°C is 331m/s. The speed of sound varies with the medium it is travelling through and with the temperature of the medium. At 20°C the speed of sound in air is 344m/s, and at 100°C it is 386m/s.

A **sound wave** requires almost three seconds to travel one kilometre. The distance of a storm centre can therefore be figured out by counting the seconds between seeing the flash of lightning and hearing the first crack of thunder. The distance in kilometres is the number of seconds multiplied by 3.

(*See also:* **C**; **Refraction of sound**; **Sonic boom**.)

Sunlight

The **light** that comes from the Sun is often called white light. However, it is really a yellowish light. Artists often call it a 'warm' light. You notice this more when the sun is low in the sky. The yellowish **colour** is, in part, because the Sun does not send waves of every length in the same amounts, and in part because the

air traps some kinds of waves more than others. The more air the light has to pass through, the more some kinds of waves are trapped (those in the blue **wavelengths**), and the yellower or redder the light seems.

When you see sunlight from a north-facing window, it is much bluer. Artists often call it a 'cold' light. (*See also:* **Afterglow**.)

▲ **Sunlight** – What we call sunlight varies depending on where we see it from. Seen from space, sunlight is far more white than seen through the dust of the atmosphere. Sunlight is yellow even when the Sun is highest in the sky, but at sunset it is orange or even red. Again, it depends on the way the sunlight is affected by gases and dust in the air.

T

Telescope

A device that produces magnified images of distant objects, such as planets and stars.

The earliest telescopes used **lenses** to gather **light** and bring it to a **focus**, but gradually **concave mirrors** became the most common way of gathering enough light. That is because a large lens is not only difficult to make but is also extremely heavy, while a concave mirror can be made lighter and far bigger.

The first telescope dates back to 1608, when it was invented in the Netherlands. News of the telescope soon reached Galileo, who built his own telescope and used it to see the planets and their moons. These early telescopes had two lenses mounted at the ends of a long tube. The length of the tube was equal to the difference between the focal lengths of the two lenses.

The **convex** eyepiece lens was introduced by Kepler in 1611. It made a larger field of view and allowed **magnifications** of over a thousand times.

Tenor

The highest male singing range. The next highest is **alto**. (*See also:* **Bass** and **Treble**.)

Timbre

The quality, or 'colour', of a **sound**. It depends on the number of **overtones** and how loud each overtone is compared with the others.

Tone

A simple tone is a pure note, such as middle C. It is produced, for example, by a certain vibration of a string or in the pipe of a **wind instrument**. However, the pure tone would sound quite dull and have little of the richness that we normally expect.

The richness is produced when the pure tone, which is called the **fundamental** tone, is accompanied by a number of other tones that are multiples of the fundamental. They are called **overtones**. If they are exact multiples of the tone, they are called **harmonics**. The fundamental tone, accompanied by its overtones, makes a pleasant **sound** and is distinguished from the pure tone by being called a musical tone.

The reflecting telescope was developed by Herschel at the end of the 18th century. In 1781 he discovered the planet Uranus using a mirror telescope. The world's largest telescopes are all mirror telescopes.

A combination of mirror and lens was developed in 1930 by Schmidt. It uses a weak 'correcting' lens in front of a curved mirror. It gives a wide field of view that is useful for looking at the whole sky.

(*See also:* **Absorption of light**; **Light-gathering power**; **Resolving power**.)

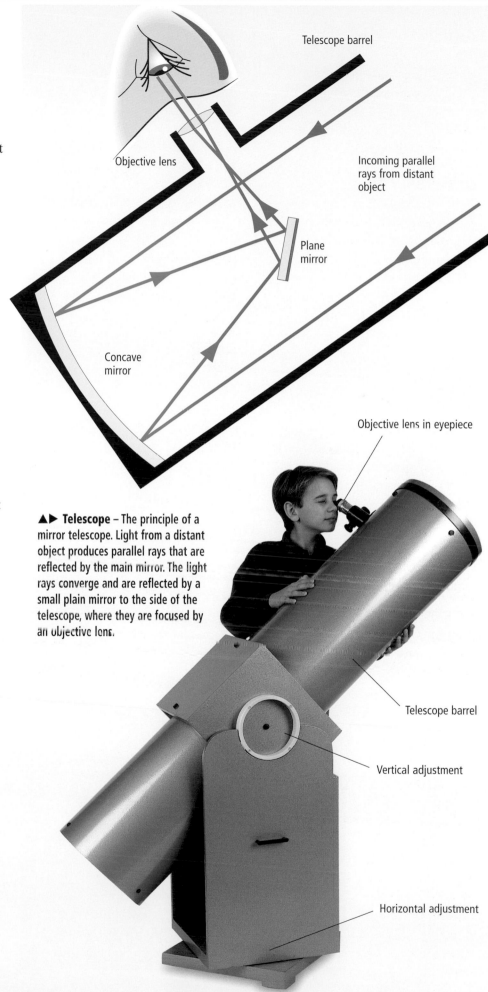

Telescope barrel

Objective lens

Incoming parallel rays from distant object

Plane mirror

Concave mirror

▲▶ **Telescope** – The principle of a mirror telescope. Light from a distant object produces parallel rays that are reflected by the main mirror. The light rays converge and are reflected by a small plain mirror to the side of the telescope, where they are focused by an objective lens.

Objective lens in eyepiece

Telescope barrel

Vertical adjustment

Horizontal adjustment

Transmitted light

Light that comes from a source, such as a light bulb (see: **Electric light**). Transmitted light has not been reflected from a surface. If it had, it would be called reflected light (*see:* **Reflection**).

Treble

The highest voice part in singing (*see:* **Human voice**) or the type of instrument with the highest range (for example, treble recorder).

Treble also refers to the upper half of the whole tonal range of an instrument or voice (the lower half being called **bass**). (*See also:* **Alto**; **Bass**; **Tenor**.)

Tuning fork

A U-shaped metal bar with a central stem. It is made to produce a particular musical **pitch** (**frequency**) and then used to help tune other **musical instruments**. Tuning forks do not go out of tune. They were invented in 1752 by John Shore.

A tuning fork produces a pure **tone** with no **overtones**. Thus, although it is useful for tuning other instruments, the tone from a tuning fork sounds uninteresting. (*See also:* **Beat**.)

Tweeter

A **loudspeaker** with a **cone** diameter of a few centimetres. It is designed to reproduce the highest **sound frequencies**.

U

Ultrasound, ultrasonics

High-**frequency sound waves**. They are beyond the range of human **hearing**. They are made by applying a voltage to both sides of a quartz crystal. That makes the crystal expand. When the voltage is taken away, the crystal shrinks again. By using a cycle of electricity, a beam of ultrasound can be produced. Ultrasound beams were first used to detect submarines. Later, they were used to map the ocean floor. The system came to be called sonar.

Ultrasonic beams can be used for many other purposes, such as removing plaque on teeth or to break up kidney stones.

Bats use ultrasound as a means of detecting their surroundings and to find food (insects) in the dark. Porpoises and whales also use ultrasound to detect shoals of fish.

Ultraviolet light

Light that is just beyond the purple end of visible light. Ultraviolet waves are slightly shorter than we can see.

V

Velocity of light

(*See:* **Speed of light**.)

Virtual image

(*See:* **Imaginary image**.)

Vision

The ability to see. The **eye** is an instrument for gathering **light** and concentrating, or focusing, it on very sensitive cells at the back of the eye. There are two groups of these cells – **cones** for interpreting **colour** and **brightness** of light, in the centre of the eye, and rods that respond to low light levels but are less sensitive to colour around the edge of the eye.

Once the light has been received, it causes chemical changes in the cells, and that in turn releases a tiny current of electricity that races along nerves to the brain, where it is interpreted as light.

Voice

(*See:* **Human voice**.)

W

Watt

A unit of power. Named after James Watt, an English engineer. **Amplifiers** and **loudspeakers** are rated in watts. A 200 watt (W) amplifier/loudspeaker system could produce a **sound level** in a room too loud for most people to tolerate. A low-power system, say 5W, would not have enough power to make the loudspeaker **cone** vibrate properly

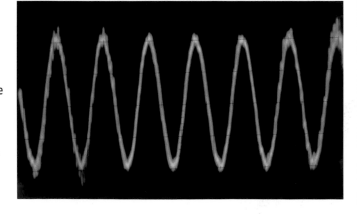

▲▶ **Tuning fork** – The sound wave from a tuning fork consists of a fundamental only. There are no overtones. So, because the tuning fork vibrates with a single pitch, or frequency, the oscilloscope shows an even, simple curve.

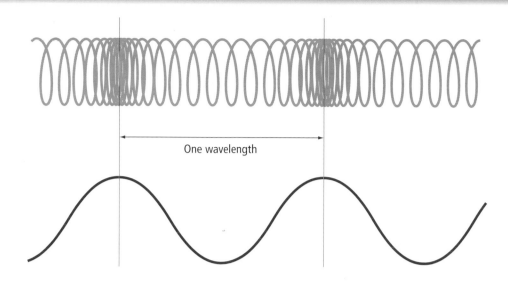

One wavelength

and therefore would not produce an accurate sound.

Wavelength

The distance between two crests (or other corresponding points) of a wave (*see:* **Light waves** and **Sound waves**). Wavelength and **frequency** are related. Wavelength is speed divided by frequency. The longer the wavelength, the slower the wave crests pass, and the lower the frequency.

Sound waves move at about 331m/sec. If the sound source vibrates 440 times a second (the note A), the distance between crests on a wave will be 331 (speed) divided by 440 (frequency) = 0.7 m (three-quarters of a metre). Using this method, it is possible to figure out that the wavelength of sound varies from 17m for a 20Hz **tone** to 1.8cm for a 20kHz tone (the normal range of hearing).

The wavelength of visible **light** is far shorter than sound waves. It is 7 hundred thousandths of a centimetre for red light, and just 4 hundred thousandths of a centimetre for violet light. All other colours fall within this narrow band. (*See also:* **Doppler effect of light**.)

White light

Light that contains all the **colours**

▲ **Wavelength** – The distance between two adjacent crests (or other similar points) on a wave.

of the light **spectrum**. It is a mixture of all of the 'colours of the rainbow'.

(*See also:* **Complementary colours** and **Dispersion of light**.)

White noise

Random **noise** over the whole range we can hear. The result is a hissing sound that drowns out all other kinds of sound. (*See also:* **Pink noise**.)

Wind instrument

Any **musical instrument** that produces a sound as a result of setting up **resonance** in a column of air. (*See also:* **Bass**.)

Woodwind

Any **musical instrument**, including flutes and **reed** pipes such as clarinets. The name comes from the fact that they all used to be made of wood. Modern woodwind instruments are often made of metal.

Flutes are made to play by blowing a narrow stream of air against the edge of the mouth hole in the flute. In the case of reed instruments the air is blown over a thin strip of flexible material until it

▶ **Wind instrument** – Blowing over the top of a bottle (right) will set up vibrations in the air within the bottle. When the degree of blowing is correct, the air in the bottle will resonate, producing a loud sound. The same principle works, for example, for a flute and pan pipes (above).

vibrates.

Woofer

A **loudspeaker** driver 3 to 5cm in diameter. It is used

Index